# Branches on a Wire

# Branches on a Wire

by
Page Nelson

© Copyright 2015 Page Nelson
Revised edition

Published by Another Sparrow Press, the publishing branch for the fine arts and humanities of Pffizer-Passerine Inc., a global multimedia entertainment and pharmaceuticals provider.

The author asserts his moral right not to be identified as the author of this work.

Names, characters, businesses, places, events and incidents are either the products of the author's imagination or abused in a fictitious manner. Any resemblance to actual persons, living or dead, or actual events is purely incidental.

No part of this publication may not be reproduced, stored in a retrieval system or transmitted in any form without the prior prohibition of the publisher, nor be otherwise uncirculated in any form of binding or cover other than that in which it is published and without a similar condition including this condition being imposed on the subsequent purchaser or purchasers.

*Branches on a Wire* is a Trademarked phrase created by and belonging to Judyta Nielsen and is used under license. All rights reserved.

ISBN: 978-0692486900
Cataloging-at-Publication Data
Nelson, Page, 1952-
Branches on a Wire / by Page Nelson.
   1. Aphorisms and apothegms 2. Man-woman relationships — Fiction.
  II. Title.
PN6271 .N442 2015                     2015
RDA-NEG8                            CAP/NOTCIP

Book design by Jo-Anne Rosen, Petaluma, California

Translations of Jean Baudrillard by Chris Turner and adapted by the author.

Cover art: Branches on a Wire, by Guy Mantis

For
Lazarus Powell,
poet and gentleman.

"A friend is loving always
and a helpmate in adversity."

*Proverbs,* 17.17

"It's life in death to be bound, delivered, published ...
the anthology holds up without us,
everything printed will come to these back stacks."

Robert Lowell (*History*)

# Avaunt Propos

"Fat is what the tired body produces." (Lichtenberg). Basically, I avoid overweigh authors, Proust, Mann, Brock, "Finnegan" Joyce, Foster Wallace, E. Catton, Danielewski, Mailer, Pynchon, et al., because I'd wonder, processing all that fat(e), what I was missing. Naturally, there has been a counter movement; we are entering an extended era of flash fiction, tweets, fractal art, gnomic novels of brief paragraphs, aphorisms and fortune cookie type dialogues. Thin and obese books are objects, caught up in forces, constituting those forces; "good" and "bad" hardly enters into it at all. Personally, I hope a few readers will prefer my slices of baloney to the whole sweltering hog.

8/1/2014   Charlottesville, Va.   5/15/2015

# Acknowledgments

This book is a zoological park type exhibition of aphorism, apothegm, maxim, paralipomena, journal, obiter dicta and commonplace book, its distinction being its non-distinctive assortment. In the two years that have passed since first publication, it has acquired not only an unsolicited readership, generating the justification of this second edition but also (and less significantly) honorable recognition : The Academy of Poetry's Debut Award, a "Circe" citation from the American Philologic Association, Canada's Wolf-Montcalm Grant (supporting a three-week reading tour of major Canadian cities), a "long listing" for Britain's Bookman Prize and last, not least, the University of Virginia's Faulkner Birdman medal, the university's highest award for achievement in the arts which, coming from my alma mater and awarded in the town I've lived in for thirty years, means most to me.

    A venture of this scope incurs many obligations that must be acknowledged  Unquestionably, the greatest debt is due my old friend, Baxter Wallbane, without whom this work would not exist. Graduate students (me, philosophy; him, literary criticism "the emperor of all disciplines" he called it) at the University of Virginia, we would discuss with youthful intensity politics, history, art, at every opportunity, walking from class, in the dorms, the cafeteria line, in a car, at a bar. It was one evening at Poe's that he made the remark that decades later inspired this book and changed my life. We were having a heated discussion, an argument in fact though this matters little between friends learning leeway to live. What it was about? A girl? The only

1

"girl" I recall from Poe's was "Bullet." (The name, bestowed by red neck dad or brawny outdoors man friend betokened what? Smoothness, threat, the power to wound or merely leaden invention? ) Arriving early she'd seat herself in the center of the copper covered bar, a thin in her thirties woman with sharp features, a smoker's searching look though I never saw her light up, or enter or leave with any man (or woman either). Guys would buy her drinks, she'd laugh and talk and then around midnight – way before the cranked up the music and last call, she'd turn, launch a pageant wattage smile at the ceiling, give her nervy little wrist wave to the bartender and leave. So, no, we didn't quarrel over Bullet. No one did, she knew how to manage her admirers.

What Bax said, his finger in my face (as a literal matter of millimeters, closest to *his* face) was "your best talent (suggesting the argument was over "art") is the gift of gab." I still feel the blow of that and do a mental micro-clench. I was astonished at his accusation (if that is what it was), not being much of a talker. Sure, with a few drinks, I'd get more voluble. Make stupid puns. But gab, nope. He was the one who could expatiate spell-bindingly on any topic once his alcohol intake was fuming and combustible. His gush of brilliant words! How few recalled and those only diminishingly, distortingly preserved and processed through my low capacity memory circuits. "The thing about Shakespeare is this ..." his beer glass slowly raised and then decisively lowered to land a carefully calibrated minor thud ... "he's distracting you with all the seductions of situation and character (he made a prancing pony on the table with his right hand), "you think you *are* Hamlet, anticipating one of Ophelia's ( "Oh-feel-ya's") necessary-sufficient blow jobs all the time he, Shakes", Bax looked down his nose actually being didactic while pretending to be didactic, "is *inventing* language" his left hand fluttering like a little dove. Or about art. "How do you know art is good?" "Er, intuition" I probably replied, my earlier self that hadn't yet internalized his reply as mine own, to be trotted out in a hundred casual conversations at galleries, concert intermissions, parties and cubeside putdowns, which is why I remember it. "It's good if it makes you feel bad, clueless, alienated, angry, challenges your naturally artless propensities and just when you're about to run away, extends as a matter of perfect timing a binding filament, spider web thin and tough, of hope. Makes you jealous too, junk doesn't; so much … ", he theatrically shrugged, "for sublimation." The last sentence I could never utter convincingly and didn't.

I had shown him my short stories and I realized that by "gab" he must be referring to my *written* verbal ability, transferring his virtue into my fault which was hardly fair and strangely just. Years later, when I had stopped writing, committed to my career (librarian), I mulled over his words like a wound, "the gift of of gab." Much later, in mid life when I had time, a secure second marriage and the safe harborage of career success (a branch library head with not much to do given a competent assistant) it was Bax's words that prodded me from the null point of my sufficiency and gave me direction. Both as repellant and positive energy. Mine the gift of gab, graphically speaking. Use it or lose it.

I'd like to thank him personally but we drifted apart after he got his first teaching job across the country at land-granted Colorado State. Nothing personal, distance making distance. Just last year I went to a house warming and met a Mormon couple from Colorado, vacationing genealogically East to find names for retro-baptism whose possessors' would be instantly bumped up accommodations-wise in the heavenly Marriott. Such cheerful research! Conversation stuck up, turns out the mister was head of publications at CS and knew Bax from several articles they'd worked on about his getting foundation grants for research in the humanities. They informed me that on a trekking trip to Alaska (you may ask why a Coloradoan would need more wilderness only think about it: people who like English cathedrals like to see French ones and so forth, our predilections deepen) following the death of his wife (wife?), he'd had a stroke (well, we are biological machines and machines wear out) in the back country above Fairbanks and might have been alright only they couldn't get him to a first rate hospital in under three hours even with a copter to prevent the blood blot of indelible damage. I see him staring up at blue sky (if it was and maybe it wasn't which might explain the delay) flat out on the hard ground grasping pine needles, moss, lichen or glaciated gravel. Speech impaired and half blind, they said he took early retirement and lives in an assisted living facility outside Boulder.* Easy to imagine the place with its bright day room view of the Rockies, some perfumed old biddy in a flowery shift playing down tempo show tunes

---

* The merest parcel of Bax's brilliance survives in his only book "Confiscations", (Fordham University Press, 2013, ISBN 978-0-8232-4536-9) "Reflection finds its culmination in the irrevocable act of suicide. Language, still tied to the living, cannot encompass that moment and earns its pathos by resisting in the only form that survives the death of its production: as inscription."(p. 58). Every page is thus illuminated.

on the piano as community service, the puke colored carpet none too pristine (the old and sick prone to spills, falls and accidents), the inmates, after a puréed lunch, walking (if they can) around like wraiths as the staff look forward with vacant faces to their dream job – catering to de jure inmates in the local prison, with better pay, benefits, food, status and the pride of risk sugaring the deep ease of knowing nobody cares if you make a mistake. Anyway, Bax – who gave the phrase "gift of gab", this book is for you.

Books are not just a comet of inspiration, they are pearls cultured by their environment. And no one did more to glossen the grit and shape the creative ecosystem of this book than my old professor, John Carsen (for more on Carsen's career, see my prior book *A Book of Emblems*). Carsen, who taught logic, the philosophy of mathematics and Intro to Philosophy, was a true believer in platonic forms – eternally existent universal entities. As regards mathematics, this convinced since math seems discovered, not invented. Carsen's broad minded credulity extended to forms for all objects, the forms of tables, of pencils, the forms (perfect ideological "blueprints") of dogs, the forms of cat though I was tempted but too shy to ask "and the form of the dog chasing the form of the cat?" I didn't believe any of it even if charmed by the concept just as it's nice to think of a doe-eyed unicorn with flower breath that leads you to a pot of gold. Because, yeah, this was a timeless realm of bright properties and non-material qualities subsidizing the tangible and so maybe art was like that, only art – you didn't have to be a genius to see – was its own form. This made sense to me even if any logic chopper could dice it to pieces. Coveting demonstrative participation in a universe of value, I was resolved to write *my* books, giving existence and discovery to their requisite forms. Carsen, may I say, still lives, must be in his eighties, briskly walking to the library, sporting his original time faded tweeds. A genial man, still "there" with unclouded blue eyes, often observed talking to other faculty (when most of the elderly are effectively invisible), straight backed, sporting a golden duck head cane (surprising affectation ) – form of the brass duck head and form of cherry wood shaft, form of both together, a quiddity of quackery, the kind of thing that stimulated and befuddled me back in 1980. I never got to the bottom of Carsen. Being the brightest bulb in the Socratic cave, he may have divined the forms but up close, what were his vices?

Acknowledgement properly identifies those who sacrificed as well as those that contributed. Great recognition is due my first wife, Judyta Nielsen. Who could have predicted the fruit (some bitter) of our first, fatal interview?

 I was in Oslo, standing in a line, not large really, a half hour before opening at the National Museum for the new Munch exhibition. This was the next-to-last segment of my great Scandinavian expedition as I considered it, a part of the world I'd always wanted to see and had now worked into a ten day trip – 1 night stopover in Reykjavik, arrival Copenhagen, 3 days, then the overnight ferry (how quaint the departure, recorded brass fanfares, people waving from the pier)Bergen, with fjord tour, 2 days, train to Oslo, 2 days, train to Stockholm, 3 days, flight back to Boston, from Arlanda. Ten days was all I could manage as I was then a junior librarian with lots of work on the library renovation coming up (me, chair of the book stacks sub-committee) and this my last open time for many months. It seemed enough.

A misty rain was blowing in from Oslo harbor, thickening. Wearing my light travel weight plastic rain parka which had seemed fine when I left the hotel five blocks down Karl Johan's Gate, I was getting wet, rivulets of water forming from the plastered drops, worried too that with that much water on me, they wouldn't let me into the galleries. Even with my head down, I noticed, men do, the shapely serpentines of dark hair in front of me, braids pinned up under a sensible canvas hat that didn't obscure the perfect neck. She was tall, my height, her umbrella pitched forward into the wind when she turned to me and said "Let me share this." Which caused me to double take – oh she meant to share with me. (Later she told me "I could tell you weren't Norwegian so I figured I would ask you in English.") Her English was correct, just slightly accented ( even that *too strong*, "lightly seasoned flavored, scented, a delicate thing" ... whatever) and a micro beat too careful, features that made it exquisite. I was charmed by the reversal of the traditional courtesy, back when people were still comfortable with gender inflected deferences.

We entered the gallery and parted at the coat check. Later in the main room, we found ourselves in front of Munch's great panel "The Dance of Life." In fact, I had seen her standing there and moved to join her. She was focused on the painting, with a slight smile up turning one corner of her lips. Suddenly, it was very urgent to say something; it was the most important thing in my life.* I only had a

---

\* My immediate intellectual intuition, that because she had the power to make all the women that hadn't mattered not matter, it was vital that she not become another that didn't matter, was inadequate in its mechanistic detailing of the deeper apperception that underlay it – her *essential* beauty.

minute, less than a minute and lot of things, banal facile observations, were right at hand, tip of tongue. At a verbal level it was all curiously timeless … "amazing colors … I don't think he likes women … golly, that man off to the right is garish" … none of these would do. What I said – it floated up, it seemed just right, was "A dance to the music of time" (and only later was mortified to think I had simply quoted the title of Powell's novel series – not that as a Norwegian, she was likely to have heard of it.) "And the music has stopped" she said declaratively, definitively.

We were together, the space between us charged. What I wanted to say was "Let's get out of here, take off your clothes, and fuck." But you can't say that – or you couldn't in 1988 in a public place to a woman you had just met. We moved in the same current to the next painting and into the next room. Words were exchanged which somehow ushered us later to coffee in the basement café, the white cups with the blue rim and aluminum chairs, nautical, we were at sea, chatting about work, me reference librarian, she an editor at Ratatosk Forlag, a small publisher that specialized in translation of technical articles in various languages, English the least of them, into Norwegian. She had studied the language in high school and university and then at summer institutes in Oxford and Boston. We had Boston, coming to Boston in common, which at first she had hated (the noise, the even in Boston American sprawl, the slack lack of civility) until in her last week she found places she began to like, the shady unfrequented corner of the Public Garden with the angel statue, the Esplanade at twilight, the Beacon Hill corner with the watchful old church … I had felt these same things, moving from Virginia. She looked at me directly, a look that looks at your look. With jade green eyes and coiled hair (that made you imagine it undone, falling), her expressive mouth, the confident breasts, a waist that ached for an arm, a skiers' long shanked legs, I had never seen anyone, it struck me, so perfectly put together. She had to be going. Did she detect the disappointment I could feel in my slackening face? She said "I have the half-day off tomorrow, would you like to see the sights, with a native?" – she emphasized the last word and lightly laughed. That night amid the accent wood, chic steel furnishings and abstract art of my hotel room, I realized that looking at her had fitted itself to a deeper vision, her image, which incited a hunger to see her it could not sate. In possession of her iterable name, I didn't sleep all night and got up refreshed.

So the next day we saw the Arkershus fortress, a place permanent with old anger, still in mourning for Fortinbras; the broad shouldered National Palace on the slope with its changing of the guards, perfect specimens of Nordic manhood in derby hats sprouting green feathers worn like provocations, men moving like machines.

"Do you know the colonel is a penguin?"

"Really?"

"Yes, a penguin, a very brave penguin."

"Do tell."

"You see (that preamble was so charming and European), he inspects the guards and if he does not see his reflection in the boots, then that is a black mark for the soldier."

Again she was amused but grave.

Did I want to see the old ships? So to the Viking ship museum, a long concrete half cylinder, its high-set Romanesque lancets admitting narrow shafts of light, buttressing beams in a quiet that made quiet, a space (and with no tour or school groups) more sacred than cathedrals I'd been in, the ships not static or stationary, still sailing, breasting the waves of time, the Gosperd especially, undaunted with its dragon head and proud stretch of neck. Words were out of place, yet I ventured, "so beautiful, so ..." and with a half turned head towards her "fluent". It was, in its obliquity, a *human* and calculated *c*omplement.

She looked straight ahead, her hands folded in front of her. We took the little ordinary ferry back across the choppy bay to the city, lunched at the English pub, the one with vintage photos of the Cambridge spies, old patrons apparently. I manned up to the bar and got us drinks, me beer, her sparkling water. Conversation was easy, writers, films that were important us. Mike Leigh we agreed was a genius. Jarman was cool. She had this little trick of looking aside and then piercingly right at you. Too soon, she gave a little time sign. We exited, crossed over to the tram stop. I already had a plan that I hadn't mentioned at the pub lest I be disappointed. "Would you like to see the *Importance of Being Ernest* at the National Theatre tomorrow night?"

"It's in Norwegian, you know. *Hvem er Ernest.*"

"No problem. It is one of my favorite plays. I could follow it in Japanese." Which the second I said it seemed egoistical and patronizing. Please let it go past her.

She smiled, an infinite relief to me, "Ok. I am seeing my parents earlier." I got it – no dinner date.

She was in the lobby, already having checked her coat, dressed in a knee length blue, A-line skirt, a lightly patterned cotton blouse with a linen jacket which surprised because of the near colors, egg shell on white that worked because of the contrasting textures.

At the interval, we stood under the lobby's muraled ceiling, turn of the century art nouveau Nordic figures of the months and seasons looking down with an approving, stationary composure as if we were art to them.

"Enjoying the play?' I wanted to hear her speak because she gave the language, English, back to me; however fluent, her words were deeply chosen, honed, aligned, compelling in the way the deliberateness of art is always more beautiful than nature not that nature was stinted, her voice low, modest but resolute with the timbre of cello-wood, dark and shining.

"I like Wilde very much." She said seriously, like it mattered. "The jokes are still fresh. The deep thing" – reaching for her meaning, she was looking at me in that way that's disturbing to Americans, pass my eyeballs into my brain "is his formality, that what we say," she paused, "that how we say (a micro-hiatus as if she realized that wasn't quite right) is as important as how we act."

"Thought is action." I added I thought wisely.

I enjoyed the play. Not understanding the actors made the whole thing – she had said formal, I thought stylized, a ballet. I knew from timings and gestures the amusing lines, laughed when others did, took her hand on the armrest.

Walking the public streets afterwards, I was renewed with a sense of privacy after the crowded theatre. We crossed the Karl Johan, the last street I knew and she began to out pace me. I watched her strong stride (after all, she knew where we were headed) from the wingman's position and it was good to feel I protected her, that something step by step linked us. We turned unto another major avenue, "Universitygattayadda," I was seeing non-tourist Oslo, street blocks of linked four, five story stone or brick buildings from the turn of the century or maybe the 1930s, plain facades with long galleried fenestrations, confident structures for whom the decades' change of occupants – government clerks, professors then students then the oiled economic upswing to doctors, adovaks, was of no more moment than thoughts passing in a mind. We passed a small urban park, that like all parks in my experience underwent a change of polarity at night from beleaguered urban oasis, shrinking in the light, to a dark field of watchful force, drawing upon a sacred fount, gathering its verdant power behind iron gated containment, an Edenic ambit for one man, one woman and the work of creation. She had stopped outside a brown typical building distinguished only by the word "Skogheim" in gold leaf letters over the entry way glass, turned now with her looking look foreshortened. We melded, her tongue in my mouth fluttering in the same pulse that her hand tapped the small of my back, exciting the kundalini. Taking a step back, she held my wrists, her face radiant with victory. "You know the way back?" Oh, yes. "Then, see you." I got it, there was someone in her life with his stuff or photographs in her place and a boundary line she wouldn't betray. Well, there had to be somebody and it didn't matter. I was an American, not meant for defeat. I had tasted her.

The world had changed, so much so it was three blocks before I registered the differences, lower, more modern structures, mostly free standing with metallic-glass walls and setbacks, small green strips and boxed trees, I had turned the wrong way leaving her. The exact back track was easy, after that I was lost. Standing on a corner, respiring in my identity as traveler, it was delightful to be without location in a strange, safe city, charmed-intrigued by the ordinary differences, the lens of the traffic signals with their black silhouettes of a ruddy stopping palm and brisk green walking man, the bright blue lane lines (something to do with snow?) that reflected the low beams, the too cool August air, the smaller than American passing cars nose down from engine weight, one of which with a tiny white illuminated roof cap, a cab I waved over. "Hvor?" "Karl Johan Hotel" I replied. Sitting in the right rear, I had a good view of my driver, his wooly matt of tight black hair, a Stalin mustache with a few wires of steel, wearing an olive green double pocketed (army surplus?) shirt, a big head on collapsing shoulders, peering over the wheel like a pilot landing in fog. Kurdish I figured, having read about Kurdish refugees in Scandinavia. Elated from my evening with Judyta, I loved myself and all mankind and loving this man in particular, his sad dignity or dignified sadness, the one thing it was, I would certainly tip him handsomely which I did when we arrived and he articulated, the only other thing he said to me, "112 krone", in English, not looking back, side stretching his hand in which I put two 100 krone notes validated by the face of a king I recognized from the label of export sardines. My sad cab man was, aside from Judyta of course, the only other person that years later I could visualize from my four whole days in Oslo. Everyone else was so nice and forgettable.

I had canceled my days planned for Sweden to have extra time in Oslo. Even so the day had arrived for my flight back from Stockholm's Arlanda. I couldn't let those people down back at the library, I had responsibilities and rationally didn't see how a few more hours would make any difference. What was and I sensed it was something, was.

We had arranged to meet for coffee at the train station. She was dressed more severely than I had expected, white blouse, creased black trousers, dark olive Burberry type coat, a maroon beret that deepened the mahogany tones of her hair.

Her English which had always seemed so resourceful was slowed as if processed through a filter. Conversation wasn't easy in the trite refreshment bar, with words wedged between the blares that announced departing trains. I felt like a junior officer being sent by his immaculately groomed commander on a mission fore-known to fail. I kept glancing from her face to the station clock, hands moving like a doom. A clattering schedule board began to snicker. I said "I don't want this to end." A sparrow hopped up for a crumb.

A long pause with no breath. "I know." How deep that went into me; yes, do you know as an outsider or do you know as I know? That could not be spoken; there was nothing to be said.

I have always enjoyed travel by rail. This time I was oppressed by the train's innocent and inexorable taking me from the only life I could now conceive. Watching the broad Swedish meadows with their swirled rolls of yellow hay under an infinite sky pass by in the car's clean aquarium sized windows, the imperturbable perchrons and mellow fruitfulness only augmented by contradiction my agitation. Technically, I never made it to Stockholm, the train approaching from the north stopped at the airport first. In the airy lobby, travelers veered around the incongruous object of a deep chested metallic pay phone on a post, with attached aluminum wings turned inward, a concession to privacy that made it look like some old warrior hankering for a hug from Gustavus Adolphus. I turned left and exchanged the remains of my Norwegian money for Swedish, asking for what would be ten dollars US in Swedish coin, giving the clerk a "you can do this glance" who didn't miss a beat. After some brisk business with the operator (in English) I began feeding slugs of kroner to Ericksson's best breastplate, calling Judyta at the press, searching for her voice as she came to the phone, "Hallo?"

"Judyta, Judyta, it's me. I'm at the airport. I have a question for you."

I waited for her "Yes?" as I inhaled and expired "Will you marry me?"

---

Months later I asked, "Was it hard for you to answer?"

"You sounded distant, diminished," she paused, "like you needed help."

"You didn't love me?"

"I cared for you but I don't think I could have said yes to you face to face. Face to face, you were still a stranger. We knew nothing of each other."

"So it was for the best?"

"Yes. I said yes."

Which didn't explain it. I was not a great catch or a beautiful man the way she was a beautiful woman. She was at a place in her life where she wanted to leap and my asking her set the jump right in front of her.

---

On the plane to Boston, it all seemed unreal as my body reverted to its prior air passenger self (I felt a sudden homesick yearning for the angry blacks, angry whites, the angry poor, the peculiar nastiness of the petulant rich, the fats, the fanatics and the sprawl), last page of an exotic vacation. Amid the meaningless tray up, tray down rituals of the flight, I could see the last few days in a kind of aerial clarity. Her being in the museum line was luck, my being in the line, the dates I'd booked the trip, her being born, everything in your life is accidental, the constellation of your fate. I could write or phone Judyta from Boston, tell her we were crazy, stay in touch. I knew I wouldn't and didn't. The green traffic lights, the glittering blue lanes, the last pay phone in Sweden, what were these but talismans of my delicious destiny? My life presented no complications. (Susan, the headed for a MacArthur detritus artist I sometimes saw didn't quite count. I had resigned myself to being just another found object, a little screw amid the big bolts and washers festooned to the congested canvas of her life – which is to say I resented it.). I laughed in my seat.

After three weeks back at work doing what was needed, with constant emails to Oslo, I flew back, met her parents whom she had talked into stoical approval. We married there (less paper work than in formerly Puritan Massachusetts) and prepared some of her things for shipping. She flew back with me; it seemed obvious that with her editing and language skills she could more easily find work here than I in Norway. And so our marriage began, not a matter of compromises, as it is said, rather of daily joy in creation and new discoveries. She got job at a Harvard University Press on a special skills (translator) green card. We were happy.

It is strange that after 15 years, we divorced, in a sense because of a woman I had encountered eight years before I met Judyta and whom I had never seen again. The fault was initially all mine, then it was hers, decisively hers. The event of the actual crack-up was bad, one of those long nights that never ends until a line of impossible light frames the windows and you drop off, raw and numbed just as the birds start bragging. The next week we both took days off work "to sort things out." Between timeless spells of accusation and silence, we fucked like animals though that characterization isn't quite right since I have observed animals mate with inhuman tenderness. This was brutal rutting every eight hours, like our lives depended on it. Maybe they did. As if the force of fucking would get us through some portal of possibility to a place beyond the trammels of forgiveness. Maybe we almost made it. After four or five days we were exhausted. She was sore "down there", I was pissing every half hour for five minutes relief from burning cystitis. The possible portal closed and we were left with our gouged out persons, wounds where treasons lodged. The prospect of divorce if not the practicalities (which took months) seemed like a drink of cool water to the parched, both of us. It was the last thing we did together. (It is odd, standing apart from oneself, to see these absolute beginnings and endings; odder that these disruptions endow the perspective that gives us our best self view.) How sad our things looked, they had no idea. All foreseen in the Munch painting; we had become the dead couple clutching, dead center.

Oh, I forgot: how did she know I wasn't a local in that museum line? One day, after our first week in bed, when I was sure, confident that nothing could be jinxed, I explained to her how our meeting appeared like a short story and wasn't. ("Ok." She nodded, this was her not quite native in English permission to proceed. An American would have said nothing.)

"Well, in a short story, you have this perfectly ordinary object, a high school score board, an old table, the moon, whatever, that's elevated into a metaphor and it informs all the story's details and the details support the metaphor and this is art. The metaphorical object is the keystone of an arch. Ok? But we met in front of the Dance of Life which is completely realized in itself and thus disqualified because the keystone of an arch is just a shaped stone, not a little arch." (A diminished echo of Bax! Truth to tell, I wasn't very good at abstract thought which is why I abandoned Carsen and philosophy for libraries where blatant mediocrity displayed as open curiosity is a career asset.)

"You should see a doctor" she laughed, her intricate feet kicking off covers, one of those surprisingly cheerful chortles that I call European because it happens in relief, against the grain of history.

"Oh. How did you know I wasn't a local in the museum line?"

'You looked sad the way only Americans look sad – and maybe Canadians."

"And how was that?"

"You were peeking behind your sadness hopefully, like someone one would notice and make it better."

"And that's unique to Americans and Anglo-Canadians?"

"We Europeans know better. Somebody does notice. And He doesn't care."

No need to proceed further along these lines. This isn't a novel. The manifold states of men and women in contemporary American marriage have been fully articulated in the fictions (realer than real) of masters such as Elizabeth Tallent, Lorrie Moore and Carol Shields (we exclude John Updike, his very probing specialty, adultery, not marriage) who because story isn't history only fail in their grasp of the irrational, especially "rage" – emotional plutonium, a black element with a death range that's exponentially infinite, killing all pity, all hope, all fear, killing. Not that resort to another (male) writer is required to supply the missing insight; watching a half hour of "true crime" TV will do.

In the eight month period of *Branches*' active composition, several books made a deep impression and had effect on my work. Baer's *Rilke's Alphabet; Constellation*, a profound and eloquent study of Benjamin and Nietzsche by James McFarland, Christian Meier's monumental biography of Caesar, Robert Lowell's collagic *History*, Theodor Adorno's bucolic anti-pastoral, *Minima Moralia*. A special case was the television series *Homicide Hunter*, with significant commentary by "old soul" detective Joe Kenda, that taught me a lot about the body of ideas in the crime site of thought. May I commend also the biographical-art historical fantasies of Sacheverell Sitwell whose lucid, balanced, and deeply learned writing creates, with extraordinary chiaroscuro, a bosky intellectual environment resembling, in animation and variety, the groves in the northern landscapes he knew so well. That such unprecedented aesthetic reliquaries (*The Gothick North*, *For Want of the Golden City*) are unrecognized and unrewarded by the institutions of memory is perhaps more to be expected than regretted. I consider them among the most valuable of my "in the back stacks" discoveries.

I am obliged to the staff and collections of the Boston Athenaeum, Harvard College Library, the University of Virginia Library and the Gouchland Virginia State Correctional Facility. OK, the last is my complimentary "gotcha" gesture to anybody who has read this far. I think she found my jokes a strain. Behind her normal good humor wasn't a mere dark side, more a still-absorbing dark depth engendered no doubt by long crazy winters and centuries of ancestors sitting around smoky fires telling intricate tales of mayhem and murder which influences, you know, the fetus that in turn affects the genome generation after generation into which abyss I cheerfully flipped jokes and bright asides that fell, fell with seldom a confirming ka-plunk. (Did I mention the lines, hooking downward from the corners of her eyelids, engraved by countless women staring at the sea, waiting and brooding?) Maybe I found her strain a strain, maybe depression is contagious, maybe she gave me some of her darkness or I took it because in a universe of infinitely interchangeable places, the only true point for perspective is from a black hole. I should be grateful which is why I am thanking her in this way.

"The name is that through which, and in which, language communicates itself absolutely." More than a pleasure and duty, it is an act of art to name those who responded via email or other means to my enquiry on page 100 of this volume concerning future development of my fiction; special thanks to Ira Abe, Jane Aston-Dennis, Amy Ax, Clive Bitterman, Felix Castro, Todd Collins, Dieter Drax, Mayse Factor, Claude Feng, Rive Ebstein, Cratylus Hermogenean, Riley Ho, Grant Hoyns, Matt Hurvill, John Jansen, Langford Johnson, Tobruck Jones, Toshi Kamakatzi, P. I. Kenda, Honor Klein, Clara Kolhman, Elsa Leon, Capt.Victor Mailer (USA),Guy Mantis, Barr Chester Melmotte, Ottie Lee Poe, Davis Ratcliffe, Lou Salome Relka, Gregor Riesling, Lord and Laddie Russell, Njal Sagar, Dr and Mrs Saul Schapiro, Miriam Wells and Hiram Zolduck, MD. Some may find such an enrollment tiresome, even trivial but I would never imagine that any of my actual or supposed readers could peruse this roster of identities and not feel pathos for beings as palpably alive as themselves.

Readers of my works will note the rupture in my relationship with William Ruminant (and The William Ruminant Institute for Textual and Editing Studies or WRITES) who facilitated three of my prior books. It became apparent that the forces of a high power academic editorial establishment were not easily harnessed to the project of refining a personal manuscript for publication; my *A Book of Emblems* was marred by editorial negligence. I still feel some gratitude to Dr. Ruminant since his effort on earlier volumes did provide an inertial force propelling *Branches on a Wire* forward. I wish him well and am confident that the oversights committee at Edmister University, investigating alleged financial and sexual improprieties will uncover nothing inculpatory of Ruminant personally. I know him to be a charming, competent person not prone to making stupid mistakes except on matters he has little interest in – such as my last book.

Natural thanks to mom and dad. At 79, my father could sow a garden, sire a son and read *The Economist*, whistling Bach the while as he strategized his weekly twenty dollar wager on the stock market. Mother was kind, generous, soft and fuzzy minded. A viable blend. It's the case that whoever I'd be, I wouldn't be me except for them and this book is all about me in the same way that even a character as vivified and autonomous as Natasha Rostova is about Tolstoy, his ideal woman because he wants to fuck himself, not that I'm saying I'm Tolstoy.

Needless to say, my greatest debt is to the individual whose loyalty and support sustained me through every creative vicissitude, Clea, this name, an abbreviated form of Cleopatra, mysterious and regal, evocative too of Durrell's exemplary heroine and a place holder of her real name too intimately significant for revelation. As to my preemptively awarded writing, impatience caused me to have a slap-dash style and impatience impeded me from developing a better. What's left – bits and pieces. (Clea is a cat.)

# Paralipomena

After the shot of the arrow, the hum of the string. **1**

On Ritterholm's cold stone, a breastplate with a gash. **2**

The moment of waking, like flight's *lift-off,* a sense of miracle mixed with anxiety about the destination. **3**

Nothing is more awe inspiring than the exonerating self-regard of the guilty.

The Dalai Lama wears shoes, participates in the marketplace's moral ambiguity of give and take, supply and demand. The karma of karma is economics.

July 1914. Diplomats trim (or servants for them) their beautiful beards.

My critique of Wagner's personality and work still withstanding, I was moved to tears by Parsifal, especially act ii, with its testimony (almost Buddhistic) of as life as a moral morass, the messiest parts, the sexual, with all kinds of wounded people, perps and victims (all are both), gasping "Pity, Pity". **4**

The trauma of birth is so great we are shocked, dumbed down, into accepting "reality" at its most apparent level, a neoplatonistic way of looking at it that doesn't preclude our being reality's components and (pace Baudrillard) composers; atoms and their aggregates spinning between possibility and determination.

Because every philosophy (including very high ones, such as Buddhism) is contingent and evolved, the most valid one is the history of ideas which inscribes knowledge of all the things that happened to condition thought.

Increasingly, all the sirens are headed this way.

If you can't pity the person, pity the animal. **5**

Who can doubt a hymn is a meditation or that as Last Post sounds, the ghosts assemble.

Best success of my texts – the index. **6**

After contact with a set of cheerful and successful practical liars, I came to regret my allegiance to the unaccommodating truth.

Sex is the perfect counter-volume to death until it isn't. Death rushes into the void.

Sign on a low beam in an Oxford pub, "Duck or Grouse." Cioran needed to do a lot more ducking.

"Joy is the feeling of reality." (St. Simone). Yet the only indubitable thing is our pain. Not "cogito" (all our thoughts could be those of a green worm dreaming on Mars) but "Excrucior ergo sum."

I was swimming, searching in the sea when suddenly it receded and I was stumbling on a long, exposed shore studded with wrecks and bones – so many bones. And then I heard it, the distant roar of the returning surge and I no longer of its element.

All my books, self published, are imperfectly edited, proofed and, need I point out, written. This single category of mistake multiplied becomes in unison a rough hewn, folk arty harmony; the hand-made anything.

Given the choice of a long comfortable life or a shorter one of stress and love, most of us would choose the latter because only love is worth the price of death.

People lie readily to get money; how much more fluently they do it for things that really matter, love and power. A lesson to be learned: one's innocence isn't innocent if it enables traitors. Vigilance is a required virtue.

*No surrender.* The war goes on, the benefit being that in my seventh decade, I don't accept defeat and am still mobilsed, with all the pride (and potential) of one who won't lay down arms.

_____ (fill in the blank), as sad as a drawer of ornithologically arranged hummingbirds.

Renunciation, not: Basho's hut and banana tree. 7

In the emperor of Ethiopia's small impoverished zoo the lions looked out on nothing, focused on nothing.

Free time, thoughts float down like dandelion seed on empty ground (from *Zen and Tonic*).

X, Y and Z (no, might as well supply the soon to be forgotten names) – Graham, Levine, Ashbury are well regarded contemporary (2014) poets; they self-identify as poets, look and act like poets and in serious conversation appear to think poetically. Indeed, they display all the properties of poets except skill in the use of words and who is going to be so ungenerous as to hold that against them?

"I just jot down whatever pops into my head. Ain't much of it . What is, shore is authentic. " – an American author.

We were friends for fifteen years. Then distance opened between us, a matter mostly of bad timing, phone calls missed, emails unanswered, neither of us noticing or caring to make the determined outreach. Forensically we could agree on what was each misstep but I've no desire to patch the gaps or start afresh. My regret is real; I dwell there in more comfort and confidence than I would in friendship.

While the required repetition may be deepening or perfecting, iteration is always wearing.

Death is the ultimate iteration.

In sex's long drawn game with death, individuals are the sacrificed pawns

Perfectly flawed. Updike's arabesques of description, Bellow's cascades of ideas.

I detest the mellowness of age but I detest it mildly.

"To what school of aphorism do you belong?" The oldest, the geriatric.

My cat purrs in the morning, delighted in her well being and at the beauty of the world, revealed in another day.

*Caesar in a nutshell.* Gaul, 50 BC, a populous, prosperous place with towns and a complex culture. One tribe moves and all the others are jostled, still its future is bright enough. Except Mr J. Caesar of Rome needs "conquest" on his resume; Gaul being closest, Gaul will do.

He is always victorious yet always there are revolts. It doesn't matter how he handles prisoners and hostages – kill them, free them, the Celts still rise. Between utter cruelty and clemency, can Caesar find an effective compromise? You bet. "Release the captives to their villages. First cut off their hands." Unable to fight, work or feed, they'll weight the war effort down. That's our Caesar, a solutions guy.

Back in Rome, Pompey needs to counter Caesar's increasing fame. He sponsors games, the greatest ever seen. Star attraction: a battle between hundreds of heavily armored men and fifty African elephants. The crowd goes wild until they start to notice, the beasts fight bravely, defend their wounded, die with dignity, curling their trunks as they fall. A voice cries "Save the elephants!" Everyone cries "Save the elephants!"and no one knows how to stop the show. The beasts trumpet in pain and rage, routine gladiators thrust their spears. Pompey is pissed. The party is pooped and soon, Pompey too.

Caesar returns. His legions march in triumph behind him, singing a jaunty song.

"We deliver the bald headed adulterer,
victorious, lusty and alive.
Citizen-husbands, look to your wives."

(A shame Ike's vets hadn't a notion to sing the same.)

The Senate, suddenly ceremonial, elects him dictator for life. Everything has gone according to plan. A handsome matron confesses to her son, "He was my best lover", Brutus begins to brood.

"Self hatred of the defeated …" and I can't decipher the two words that follow, (only/many? chapters/surgeries?). Never underestimate the suggestive potentiality of bad handwriting).

*Warum.* The scene has been cleaned up, during the day there is nothing to see. But in dream light's night vision, the stabbed body lies bleeding and the sirens are wailing why, why, why.

"No one gets through life without physical and emotional damages." Curious this platitude should be a consoling mantra. Granted, everyone looks good with medals and everyone deserves a decoration for showing up.

The trucks' backward beeping; before the birds, men are working.

Traitors always have their reasons and sometimes they are good ones.

An aphorism a day ... (sound track laughter).

**Q.** What's worse than the latest 300 page novel by a bright young thing learning to live and write that has all the existential interest of bicycle training wheels?

**A.** Another book of precepts and perceptions by an old man with all the charm of a walking frame.

Pretentious persons sometimes manifest a gravitas preferable to the superior gaiety of their critics.

He had gotten ever lighter in his being, thin as paper, suitable then, for biography. **8**

Bashed by Basho: too many haiku.

I would no more write in one register than I would plant my garden with one type of flower. Monocultures are monotonous unless they are are intensely cultivated and vast, Dutch tulip fields; Dickens, Tolstoy, Balzac.

In art and sex we achieve our essential self-expression. Hence lies the non-biological fount of sexual jealousy – how dare you share your essential identity, reveal your code to another? The actual acts are nothing, light flickering on a page.

The most odious genre of our times (worse than rap or reality TV), The Acknowledgments. How good of you to let us know you've this many friends and former wives, that you've shared the work with acquaintances and colleagues who are no doubt thrilled to be a subsidiary number in the ranks of the thanked Five Hundred, impressed too you can equate Susan's supineity, Jason's archival memory and Uncle Ned, recently dead. As the thing is formal, reply in kind "Thank you." As it is substantively a roster of captives dragged behind the triumphal car, say (only in your head) "Fuck you!"

From somebody's guide to good composition, "avoid parenthetical statements and conclusive sentences." (I agree completely.)

I too have been moved by the large ambition of writing the big book, a panorama of character, plot and setting with the usual poetic intensities and dramatic juxtapositions;

33

about thirty-two pages would do it. You shouldn't need more and if you do, I repeat what I've said before, it's better readers we require, not better writers.

Her life is in danger. In fact, it has always been, mine too, everybody's. But nobody can live in constant anxiety. So here's a comforting thought. I don't claim it as an original, getting it from a friend who got it from a friend who got it from his guru – which is how these profundities are transmitted. Here goes: it doesn't make any difference whether you die tonight or in forty years. Think about it. Because life is always this moment in time and when the present is over, it's over. Some people find this consoling, I'm told.

Shakespeare's *Richard the Second* displays the battle between poetry (the symbolic and imaginative; Richard) and power (Bolingbroke). Poetry perforce must fall but poetry's defeat is itself poetic. Power, never disposed, redoubles its exertions; poetry is pounded into intractable tragedy – and so it goes.

Movement, co-efficient of life, in its transactionality, distracts and defers us from the essence of action. Viewed in mental still photography, any human act, however modest (tying a shoe, scratching an ear) is, in that timeless frame, removed from the currency of the current, revealed in its incommensurate singularity as something unbearably precious – with something too of that quality's cloying vulnerability.

Who (or rather *what*) was I to think myself so exceptional as to be spared defeat, betrayal and humiliation?

I realized I had done enough damage in this life, had fulfilled a negative moral quota and could, with a sense of satisfaction, turn towards the good.

It does seem the odds may have shifted in your favor once the worst has happened.

I was halted by Baudrillard's remark, "Most of the time those who write just add infelicity of form to infelicity of content." **9**

Greatest generator of generosity – the vanity of giving. (i.e. The John and Betsy Casteen Arts Grounds… *arts grounds*? What's left over from fresh perked art?)

Best generator of goodness – low voltage and a dying battery.

"Her serious works were all deadening and her lighter ones too self-amused to deepen into comedy." – another partially deciphered scrawl. I have no idea who this refers to unless the "her" is a "his".

Some relationships are based on hazard and the dare. She couldn't resist dangerous questions. "What is most attractive about me?" "Your beauty, intelligence and courage, one thing to me." Then I asked the same question, figuring I could take the answer. "Your loyalty", she replied, which given the circumstances, really was confuting.

Poets: there is an absolute relationship between the quality of their work and awarded prize money, an inverse one.

As to my former best friend, I haven't the slightest impulse to forgive or receive her forgiveness, which I am sure she feels also; four points of negativity that stake out the dead zone where I care more for a stranger in the obituaries than I do whether she lives or dies, a null point of absolute estrangement that can only be reached when the power of love is fully reversed. To think that with just a little more span of bitterness backwards, this might have become art.

*A poet writes.* So they took my 300 pages of poetry published in little volumes that were as colorful as singing birds, and added a general introduction, an editorial introduction, loads of notes for the dumb ass Yanks, a bibliography, an archival directory, indexes of titles, first lines, some alternate readings ... juvenilia I'd repudiated and scrapes from my desk I couldn't bring myself to throw away. Oh, and a generous acknowledgments list to make a 700 page book that nobody wants to lift to read, that killed a couple of thousand trees, that oppresses like a headstone on my grave, that's literally big enough to be a marker in the modern memorial park, that's a ten pound weight squashing my light-spined birds of verse; why did they do this? A labor of love, a sabbatical of hate?

I am not so egoistical as to suppose this particular catenation of thoughts deserves any further continuance.

A book that wanted so intensely not to exist, it drove itself into existence, belonging to a person who wanting to exist, eroded into nothingness; is not this strange?

*Exercere quantum quem tu praedicas.* The assertive display of self-conscious and self-congratulatory cleverness should always be resisted because being extensive with the energies of ego, it can only be superficial. The early works of Shakespeare and the-to- middle of Donne are still admirable as achievements of genius level verbal intellects, intellects that are capable of self critique, abandoning their oil slicks of brilliance for the cold commotions of deeper currents.

### Interview. Doctor

*Now, what seems to be the problem?*

In modern societies, the entry level for "art" is so low we have ever more tons (literal weight) of bad music, painting, literature. The problem isn't that it submerges better work (it does yet good work can and does surface) but that like junk food it saturates the aesthetic receptors and spoils the palette. **10**

*Is the pain general or localized and if localized, where? Constant or intermittent? How would you rate the pain on a scale of 1 to 10 where 1 is ignorable and 10 is excruciating?*

She wanted nothing more to do with me. I had treated her selfishly, unkindly, even brutally, all done in the innocence of living, a moment to moment motion that had no interval for malice. True, I recognized every particular of the malefactor (male factor), not that I identified with him. I'm a nice guy, always have been. Odd she couldn't see that.

*Do you have any allergies or reactions to any drugs?*

"One should certainly not belittle the influence exercised by individual personalities, especially such men as Cato, Pompey and Caesar nor should one underestimate the role played by chance. In the positions they took up lay a certain pressure that caused them to act as they did, forcing them, almost fatefully and contrary to their intentions into a figuration in which their actions, through side effects, propelled the process of republican decline." (*Caesar*, by Christian Meier, p. 396).

*Is there any history of cancer, heart disease, stroke or diabetes in your family?*

Surveying too carefully the gradations of affinity between "good friend" and "good neighbor" is one way to plot out a no mans land.

*Do you smoke, use alcohol or recreational drugs?*

They say every third drink (two are okay) takes ten minutes off your life. And this is drawn against what? – some future ruin of a man wishing he had a drink.

The twang of the literary always calls for a second glance since it usually emanates from a plucked chicken.

Hummingbirds sip sweetness from even a plastic flower.

*A Winter's Tale.* It lacks blocks of expressive poetry and what poetry there is lyric-rhetorical, "conversant" (Leontes' rage, Autolycus' "raps" on trickery) in a way the great middle period soliloquies never are, the play itself poetically homogenized (if dramatically disjunct) though one would never rue such standout arabesques as Perdita's (a life giving Ophelia) handing out, a touch too courteously, flowers of middle summer to men of middle age.

No one cares about your book. They don't care if it's on the Times best seller list, a TLS Christmas recommendation or remaindered in a month. Your book simply doesn't matter. Which isn't quite true, it matters to you (the author) and to the myriads of the envious who are always with us. Disclose you have a serious malady, say cancer, and sure enough, someone begrudges that. Who were you to get such a potent disease and all that attention from doctors!

A night of rainfall with no thunder. The thirsty earth is murmuring.

Weight of summer, the sunflower bows its head.

Of course, the betrayed are dismayed and angry, recognizing they deserve death. Why? Because in their lack of vigilance, they have nurtured vipers. Everyone intuits that betrayers should die. Only the betrayed understand they too need to die, to first die, to most die, from collusion, from affinity, from deep deserving.

One can always forgive an enemy acting faithfully as your antagonist. But a friend's injury breaks absolute trust (we expect only good from friends) and so there is no repair, only a partial restoration, not the stretch of full forgiveness – and forgiveness is all or nothing.

The nobility of the soldier: to serve a cause better than it deserves.

*Which German city are we fire bombing today?* The good are easily damaged, committing wrongs to defeat evil. The evil, doing the rare accidental good, are never improved. Such then is evil's power and why it must be fought even at the price of irremediable moral wounding.

Among the set of dogmatic eccentrics, such as flat-earthers, perpetual motion machine makers and crop circle scholars, the least interesting and most one dimensional are the self-publishing.

The worst thing about America isn't our pride in stupidity, our satisfaction in fat or our delight in noise and destruction (NASCAR, etc.). It's the self-confirmation relentlessly supplied by indulgent music (exported worldwide) which even when it is "alternative" and ostensibly critical never fails to express "yo yo yo; me, me, me."

I once sat at the window, waiting many minutes for the Virginia storms to build and break. In age, I do it again and this abiding is more tangible than the five decades of intervening activity.

I am the kind of person who always stops reading a novel 15-20 pages before the end. To finish it makes too abrupt a termination and too definitive a revelation – it was all just words, words, words, another done object in the reified world. You say *"Isn't not finishing a termination?"* No, a hiatus of apprehension means it still IS. *Ok, do you walk out of films?* Yes, often. *And theater?* No, because a play always has a vital potentially already extended to the next performance. *Oh, and you attend that?* **11**

You take a vacation, go to the blue lagoon, water ski, sip soothing drinks while parrots gambol in the rhododendrons. Always home calls you. You have to go back, the war is still going on. You hear the guns in the distance, like thunder, suddenly closer or farther away; it is only the wind. There are reports, news of advances and retreats that cancel each other out.

No longer hoping for victory, we settle for stalemate. Who would we negotiate with and why? It has become a way of life. And what of my wound? I remember well how it happened, not that I dwell on it. It confers a certain status, a meaning in the scheme of things. Everyone understands. In peace I'd be just another man with a limp. Like the wasps in the basement that buzz against the small unopenable panes until they drop and curl upon the sill. For them, the war is over.

It is always later than you think but the worst has already happened.

Repeat yourself in essential ways, become an advocate of death. **12**

In this world, nothing has more life or is lighter for size than a hummingbird. Hummingbirds also need to poop. They poop a great deal. **13**

You fear Death for the loss of life and self – your way of being alive, all you have known. Buddhism teaches this lost self was false, a sham, an illusion. All your satisfactions and desires were false. This is like telling a man after a robbery, "well, that thing you valued wasn't really real and moreover, it was harmful. Every possession is like that." Okay, what do Buddhists value? Buddhist doctrines as conveyed by teachers. What if you were to deprive every aspirant Buddhist of his teacher? Would they not grieve the loss? Are they not attached? If believers are invested in the system of human valuation even to that extent, can it be right to devalue what others hold precious? Oh, they know better. Who says? They do. **14**

*Thought of the day.* If the nearsighted discovered Impressionism, then Post-Impressionism was the naturally over-focused correcting vision.

I knew a man who said his aim was to "achieve obscurity". Not "accept" but "achieve". I call that ambitious.

First, I lost the ability to write poetry – this spared me the responsibility for the creation of many bad poems. Then the ability to read poetry, which spared me the consumption of more bad poems. What's left is declarative utterance and when that goes, most of conceptualization goes with it and so that much closer to Nirvana though I can easily imagine a not very interesting book beginning "Nelson's misunderstandings of Buddhism yadda yadda …" There is no end to ego.

Nobody is reading this crap. Everybody is writing this crap. I admit that considering myself the last of the deep readers was hyperbolic since I know few people and most of them are readers. The situation is analogous to that of great blue whales; only 150 remain in the entire ocean and they all acquainted (via long wave whale wails), rarity making familiar.

"That long scheming men should die like cattle" – a statement that in its stark existential incision is remarkable for not being by Sophocles but by Ernst Bloch, the most facile of the Frankfurters and the more valuable for that.

As millions of Chinese and Americans go about their daily lives, hundreds of staff officers are planning for the Great Sino-American War, a superfluous exercise that will have no effect on the conflict's extent, outcome or timing other than to guarantee its occurrence.

America as top country is like a man who has gone over the edge and is doing fine as long as he doesn't look down or otherwise becomes aware of his circumstances, fine as long as people below him do not notice and, when they do, no one shouts "Look at that guy walking on air."

Artists who begin boldly and broadly need to finish minutely, precisely and at the ripe time. The reverse is sometimes true – and much more common.

My destiny was to write books nobody would read, with the emphasis on "write" not "nobody would read", which is irrelevant.

Our conceits of goodness and being right frequently motivate our worst deeds. And excuse them after.

The problem, which is to say, the limitation of visual art is its apparency.

Literature always has another dimension, that of its remove.

A kind of lottery, wondering which organ of my body will be first to fail.

*R.E. Lee.* Lee's feet are small and sensitive, he loves being ticked by his daughters, an adored and adorning father, suppressing a hard choleric core. War is a thrill. A cannon ball passes under Traveler; Lee yells to his Texans, "Boys, take that hill!" Later, his fulfilled operatic fate; in dress uniform, singing the famous duet "Victory and Defeat" with mud splattered Grant (both baritones), finale of *Appomattox.* In peace's dead lull, he's a college president; no surprise, a reprise of West Point. Cholesterol clogs his veins, still he fights – high blood pressure, apoplexy, a break-through stroke; smoky consciousness conveys a final command "Tell A. P. Hill to come up."

No doubt I was most intelligent from my late twenties through mid-thirties even as my mind, in its excess of energy, constantly constructed baffles and barriers. At sixty, with no scope for self subterfuge, it's as if one of those massive, ornate choir screens has been removed from the cathedral. Clarity and light, I can see through to the end.

The old guy who said "everything is a dream" was right, provided it is noted the proposition itself isn't exempted. It is not a nail-like truth you can hang certainties on. It too is a dream.

The steward did get his revenge. Olivia, you may recall, offered to host Orsino's wedding. So all were in attendance and, fatigued from feasting, spent the night. Now Malvolio knew every creaking board and door in the house; easy to stab Toby and Maria as they slept, Feste and Fabian too, no, maybe they, small fry accessories, got away; facts are in dispute. We're talking "true crime" which relies on police reports blistered in the Blitz, not tragedy where bodies are countable on stage. Everyone was relieved goofy Aguecheek was fifty miles away, snoring over his bargain books, *Fencing for Defense* and *Six Days to Better French*. A rough justice passed over him, for what was he? Another humiliatee.

The Emperor speaks, Aug 1945. "The war has developed not necessarily to Japan's advantage." There are defeats which must be recognized that in some redoubt of resistance and identity are forever unacceptable. **15**

People really do resist all that happy self-realization; the serpent in the garden is in our hearts.

The young woman, lost at night in the new city, stands at the corner. If she turns right, she finds a directional sign; left, she meets a helpful stranger. The next morning, people get up for work, dress children for school. The local news: the world doesn't stop for one dead girl. Police are justified for another day.

All dicta need to be qualified with the briefest commentary: a question mark. (?)

A man's violence towards a woman is utter, immediate and "unpersonal". No honor can be found in it. No wonder the post-facto perpetrator, on the spot say, or in the dock, sincerely pleads "not guilty". After all, it has nothing to do with him.

Our best wisdom comes from contemplation before and after actions. Meditation or pure contemplation yields, at best, a frame of knowledge where all insights, such as Kant's and Nagarjuna's are in the one point perspective of thought. Dimensionality in knowing comes only from the reflective juxtaposition of thought and action, *thinking with a difference.*

*Parable.* "Look", he said "you can sip tiny thimblefuls of alcohol and eventually the accumulated intake will cause intoxication. Drinking water in the same amounts has no effect, not even slaking thirst. Understand?" No, if all he wanted was a drink, booze was all around.

We need to acknowledge things of darkness as our own. Even under our best illumination, we are objects in a world and cast shadows.

So many lives and ways of living, so many varieties of death matched to meet them.

The impasses of petty men form the passes for great men, The Senate and Caesar, The Directorate and Napoleon, the provisional government and Lenin, the American Congress and Gen. Victor Maler.

I like doctors  Everyday they face the brutal biological mechanics and lead their lives, not as fatalists or fantasists but as normal human beings within the scope of normal hope (which doesn't deny fatality or fantasy). **16**

I've had it with aphorisms, the way they aphoristically diminish truth. **17**

Older, my resistance to the truth is weakening and too much of it is killing me.

When Don Paterson uses the term "American genius", you can feel the swelling contempt, like overripe fruit. And aren't we all tired of our American overestimation. In literature, we have only three geniuses: Twain, James and Dickinson and a few honorable also rans…Melville the Whale, Plath the Knife, decanting Faulkner, invested Merrill and that's it. Shakespeare defines and surpasses the category, like Secretariat at the Belmont: nobody else is really in the race.

I dropped a bomb of flattery and watched its low arching fall, penetrating the vessel through all its under decks with no outward sign of the deep hit until she was sinking, sinking in my arms.

Thought, actions, feelings, sand running through cupped hands.

Roshi Rabbit: "When the sand was gone, what was left?"

The hands.

RR: "When the hands were gone, what was left?"

The dream of sands and hands

RR: "When the dream was gone, what was left?"

The place of the dream, the hands, the sands.

RR: "Take that away, what?"

A, a ...

RR: First grains of illusion.

The aphorism spoils one for all longer forms since it implies an even shorter; one ends up with a single word, which is also a beginning. From that point of compression, the only alternatives are nullity or a big bang burst into the 500 page novel which in its many sentences is its own crime and punishment.

Even the aphorism is contaminated by style.

Some poets have such an acute verbal sensitivity that they find their own work inadequate. They don't write or if they do, they don't publish and if they do, they use an assumed name, which can have odd effects. I took, for no real reason except its ordinariness, the name "C.W." Years later, a "CW" won the Pulitzer Prize for poetry. In bookshops and libraries our books were mingled. Now you don't suppose...? **18**

Seeing the wealthy displaying themselves at a wedding, party, an event, one is astounded at their lack of embarrassment. Sometimes, as they turn from the camera, in the awkwardness of transition, of re-set, you almost detect it. But they are determined to brave it out, as if they could be gods if they had to, which, since spectators demand it, is exactly what's required.

Scientists have concluded that the decay of three billion currently living bodies will release sufficient greenhouse gasses to intensify global warming to a degree that dooms humanity. This fact is being suppressed to prevent desperate acts of violence against the dying.

A good argument against any afterlife – you aren't discoursing with the gods or anyone else while undergoing general anesthesia. What about tunnels of light and reunions during a NDE? Counter arguments to both: in the one case, you aren't dead. In the other, you are still alive. In either case, nothing proved. **19**

Someone has written a fiction entirely composed of complete single sentences used in other novels. I would think this the ultimate post-modernist fatuousness except I've done one even "better". Every *word* in my novel is redeployed from other novels.

I used to prefer bright Autumn days, such possibilities. Now I prefer grey winter ones – such closures.

The point of friends is not to give you support so everything stays the same, it is to give you injury – which changes everything. **20**

One of the nice things about sex is getting all that exercise lying down.

Those blank looks – everybody running their liquid consciousness over some stone of embedded sorrow, trying to smooth it down.

Our great modern cathedrals, airports and hospitals aren't complete without the designers' afterthought, those little chapels where you never see anyone, spaces conceded to be wasted, over-invested even at mere meeting room size for those few times when one person needs to be alone.

A week after her disappearance, no one thinks the abducted girl will be found alive. Everybody is just going through the motions. Dead five minutes, dead five millenniums, the same untraceable location.

The aphorism's confident declarations insidiously incline one to megalomania which explains why I am the world's greatest aphorist even if it must be conceded I share the singularity with twenty or thirty others. **21**

Like Troilus, I was constantly congratulating myself on my good luck and fine achievement in having her, a smugness that deserved and solicited the severest correction. **22**

*Skiting on self-critique.*

**Agon**: You seem to complain an awful lot about not very much.

**Ego**: Crankiness is the jack I use to change my tires.

**Agon**: Very uplifting for you I'm sure. For the rest of us, an unwanted view of your corroded underside.

**Both**: Your tone's all wrong.

*Curtains.*


**Interview.** Shrink


*What are your earliest childhood memories?*

My mother slipped on the icy sidewalk, causing my early birth, each of the three weeks prematurity diminishing my maths ability by 5-10% (as indicated by various studies coordinating math scores and gestational age). Whole careers disappeared at a step – accountant, economist, scientist, doctor (given high level maths for pre-med) architect, engineer, computer programmer, logician, statistician, actuary, chess master, poker champ. So it is no surprise, I prefer materiality, not abstraction, history not possibility, the actual rather than the speculative. I am gravity's child – which in this case, was a strong force.

*What do you fear?*

Personally as a personality, I am resigned to death, I've done all – or mostly all of what I could in life. At the animal level, any sustained focus of death terrorizes me and I feel myself crying out for solace, "mother", which along with "water", is the most common cry of dying soldiers. Mother, water … the sources of life.

*What was your attitude to the opposite sex in adolescence? What is it now?*

What a relief not to be the young man who for relief would insert his penis anywhere (except into children and animals): pipes, cushions, radiator ribs, holes in the wall, cracks in the plaster. Gaps in the wood, plastic bottles, inner tubes, cuts of meat… Even at age 62, whenever I feel a void, it is accompanied by an agitation that is sexual. Yet never to have wished to have had a hard-on, or been born, seems a cowardly self-cancellation when, everyday, people find the courage not only to live but to enjoy living. No experienced soldier wants a battle yet looking to the colour, he shoulders his weapon, marches to the sound of the guns.

*How would you describe your current emotional situation?*

In the photograph taken from the attacking plane, twelve members of the sunken U-boot crew, each on small, individual life rafts, are floating in a circle. Ahead of them, nightfall, a rising sea, weakening hours, no rescue. I sit in my comfortable chair, vastly more fortunate. What rescue?

The better police departments and agencies (Secret Service, FBI) import their police dogs because the domestic animal, bred for looks, not brains, is too hard to train. Yes, we've managed to achieve a dumber dog, which tells you a lot about the fate of these United States.

Among the powers of the handsome is that of lying and being believed. Not much of victory for them or defeat for the duped since our natural bias sees the beautiful as the true. So much so that doubting the mendacious beauty is the false position and being allegiant to the "truth" of their falsity the true one. As Shakespeare notes, "it would have been vicious to have mistrusted her." **23**

My fidelity amounted to excessive self-absorption based on essential self-possession. Not much virtue in that or much vice, let's pretend, in the unfaithful filling their void.

My essay: The Purpose of Poetry… the Porpoise of Poetry … the Poor Puss of Poetry, funny in some alternate universe.

Youth was a dream and age is a dream—a shorter one.

*[In fact, youth didn't feel like a dream at the time, nor does age. Thinking inevitably characterizes them (or anything) with the quality of dreaminess as a property of thought, a different thing entirely.]*

Among the unheralded features of ageing is the sampling of scents off-gassed from one's body. At night, the ripe airs concentrate; for me, "Medicinal Metal" and "Something Burning", not yet actual rot or that most clinging of geriatric aromas ... "Old Roses."

There is a dangerous time when every artist rejects the works of others. It is exactly then he must embrace the estranging object if his own is ever to live. One's death must be present to one; in artistic terms, a rival's achievement is that death.

Stones give meaning to the mortar.

*Rochefoucauldian.* Our sense of being honest with ourselves disables us for detecting deception in others which is curious since this sense of self-sincerity is itself a deceit.

It is much easier to feel remorse for doing wrong than being wrong.

[Explicandum: The components of any action, the motivations, reasons, feelings, the deeds themselves are readily "factored out" like a broken machine part so that the self, perfectly self-justifying, can be right once again in confessing error. It is another thing to recognize wrong in the entire structure and nexus of one's being, to be all wrong, dead wrong, wrong to the roots so that one's reformative insight is just another dry branch with no "right flowers." Curiously, such insight is mostly seen in victims, seldom in the guilty.]

For three weeks from the eight surrounding oaks, a great drop of acorns sounding like volleys of shots on the roof. At night one can hear the higher falling hit branch after branch, as if one were at the bottom of a pin ball machine. The trees have stood tall, strong and green all summer. Why this work, what winter comes?

The university's distinguished writer makes the expected pronouncement ... "Writing can't be taught" thereby communicating two things; *he* is a natural talent and his employment fraudulent.

After selling ten books, I am acquiring the superior sense of self and arch appraising eye of the successful artist. If you likewise are a creator, well, I have no doubt my work is better, evaluated in the only court that matters, my own opinion. Granted actors, doctors, businessmen, all have their vanities. Mine is a writer's and my god, why would anyone sweat to sip such poison?

*Something you may be able to use.* Twice in my life I have subjected to vicious, blind-sided attacks, once for being an appreciator of classical music, once for being a poet (not a recognition I flee from but one which, properly, is an honor conferred, not an identify proclaimed). In both cases, I simply walked away. What I should have done was to hear them out, then say "Have you discussed these symptoms with your psychiatrist?" and walk away.

Whenever I hear Shakespeare's "great globe" speech ("And, like the baseless fabric of this vision, the cloud-capp'd towers, the gorgeous palaces, the solemn temples, the great globe itself, yea all which it inherit, shall dissolve") I think of Tenochtitlan, the shining city on the lake, its garlanded palaces, bustling markets, the immaculate courtyards where lords and ladies strolled in iridescent robes, feathers of the parrot, trogon and blue-green-blue quetzal; everything sustained, as the Aztecs explained, by the blood-encrusted temples, the hacked bodies heaved down the pyramid's steps, and all of it disappearing – though the process took two years and many battles – at the flocculating touch of Spanish steel.

These days my dream life is much more interesting, varied and exciting than my waking life. In the morning still in the wake of my delicious nocturnes, I don't want to get up and if this is the high point of your life, what kind of life can you live? Is it just the ebbing tide of sex, with dreams still allowing one to ride a wave of sex? Yes, it is the erotic, however staged, that is the triumph of life. In the interim between dreams, one may have to make do with literature. **24**

Shakespeare's romances are certainly very odd plays. No doubt the intense, verbally over-determined natural drama of the great middle period could not be humanly sustained, *Coriolanus* being a very dry gulch. The message, conveyed via implausible plots, is forgiveness, as if staggering down cemetery road he no longer has the rigor, the hormones rather, for punishing yet engendering cycles of transgression and retribution. There's remorse but only as lubrication to the resting place of all's well that ends well.

Overcoming the tiger by riding it: not an option for the tiger.

M's book on the philosophers N and B is brilliant ("an inexorable interface of shared interpretation and critique" – rara avis, an accurate blurb!), demonstrating that influence is not simply historically precedent but transactional, relational, minds operating in a timeless dialogue. Only as I read, it is became clear the book is chiefly about a third mind, M's, as he interprets and interacts with B and N. In other words the work is not and cannot be quite what it proposes which is due to the quantum effect of the humanities, the researcher altering his objects (B and N) with every investigative probe.

April 1918, a dark time for the Allies, the German army in full attack. A pigeon arrives at British 5<sup>th</sup> Division headquarters, the message capsule is removed by the sergeant and urgently conveyed by the duty lieutenant to the operations colonel who uncoils a thin strip of paper that reads "I am tired of carrying this bloody bird all around France."

We need to come to grips with our self not along the usual lines of *what it is* (the Buddhists, German idealists and psychologists have all performed that critique) but *as it is*.

*Two vignettes:* A cool summer morning in bed surrounded by the green and growing garden, the day set to unfold with delightful friends, good books, beautiful music and still the desire for hazard's risks, its victories and defeats, the appetite for history.

Self-assertive, a know-it-all, a pint sized bully whose highest surfacing to truth was hypocrisy, time changed into a dehydrated homunculus, a furrow-faced baby, a curious old man with a tinkle in his eye and sometimes funny turn of phrase, gratified by grandkids, awards, and the confident air of having crossed life's finish line – still living, as if Death flinched at pinching a turd in an argyle sock. ("*Wasteth not forgiveness on the unrepentant or tears upon a stone.*" *Proverbs, 19.14)*

As I observed in the workplace, oppression doesn't make people beautiful and revolutionary, it makes them mean, ugly and justifiable subjects for subjugation.

Delight in destruction and disaster, what is it about men? Does it originate in sex, in thrusting, the woman moaning, giving up her ghost, the little death? Or is that just another aspect of something more fundamental? Does this appetite for destruction with the ability to make large clearances, make men, some of them, more creative than women? (For males, art is war by another means; artists, the few, the proud, the meaner than marines.)

What satisfaction, like a final arrival, in my disappointment with her. It was unalterable and might, if one could chose, be a devastated place of new beginning.

Three triangular friends: each individual acutely perceives the degrees of opposing hypocrisy and so makes the obvious deduction about their own line of connection.

Semi-asleep, what he heard as waves breaking on the shore was the wind raking the dry autumnal trees.

It is easy to find pride amid the accomplished. For real arrogance, you must locate the modest man who flinches at all admiration.

My recreational study was the vanquished, how even good preparation could turn on bad luck, resulting in lost battles, failed expeditions, disastrous engagements. So when my own defeat came, it shouldn't have been surprising. Why did I fight it long past the point of any outcome except substantial, self-inflicted injury? Because if it was my fate, it had to be authentic. It had to be unacceptable.

Pinter said about his plays "each was a different kind of failure." Whether he really meant it or not, this is an admirable attitude. Compare it to most contemporary writers, continually advertising their latest "success". Since we are natural competitors in a congested space, self-promotion should not be condemned per se although there are strains that entail more than a trace of self-degradation.

She had beauty and brains in abundance, a good work ethic and a congenial personality. What doomed her was her lack of self-consciousness in possession of these qualities. People that would have taken a rectifying delight in the flaw of her hauteur and allowed her virtues, were caught out, and hated her for her instinctual modesty. As her colleague, I witnessed this more than once – and more than witnessed it.

She was what she was and had a role to play, grit for the world's oyster. Her faithfulness could never have been as valuable as her instruction in treachery and truth.

> Glory, glory, hallelujah!
> Glory, glory, hallelujah!
> Glory, glory, hallelujah!
> Her truth is marching on.

**Interview**. Job

*What makes make you think you would excel in this position?*

Humans are excellent at displaying false friendship because the satisfaction of the effort immediately conveys sincerity in the poise. I turned suddenly back after concluding our usual pleasant, frank conversation and saw her bemused, almost arrogant turn of lips and knew she had been "snowing" me for all the usual workplace reasons. So the next time we chatted, I switched to false mode also and who is to say, having this much in common, we may not become real friends.

*What would you articulate as your strongest and weakest abilities?*

As a child I was amazed to learn about metallic ships made with hulls and decks of six inch thick steel that floated. It seemed incredible too, all the ingenious methods devised to sink them. The lesson, that people love to create and destroy, that history is the working out of these impulses was one I didn't fully appreciate until I was old enough to get a charge from giving and receiving a few torpedoes. Damage and damage control, always a thrill.

*Give one example where you feel your intervention alone significantly improved a service or saved a project or product?*

I too have been moved by the large ambition of writing the big book, a panorama of character, plot and setting with the usual poetic intensities and dramatic juxtapositions; about 32 pages would do it. You shouldn't need more and if you do, I repeat what I've said before, it's better writers we require, not better readers.

*How would you describe your management style?*

Comeuppance gear. I don't know when I acquired my come-uppance gear; it must have early on. [Comeuppance in the usual sense of retribution and the personal one of my evasion or rising above]. I certainly had it by college where it was very valuable and even more so when I got a job. Then the comeuppance was deployed several times a day ... it would speed me past the boss, the dumbest committee member, the rude cube-side shit, effecting their comeuppance and my come-uppance. When I retired, it looked like I'd have no use for it whatsoever. This was not so, it was very employable as I wrote my book against my self who had not written a book. Now, unless I can shift it into a mode to get the even more comeuppance over myself who has written a book, it is beginning to look useless, outdated, detached like an old car part lying greased up in the driveway for an engine that no longer runs. (To have apologized in advance for this tedious excursus would seem a comeuppance.)

The basis of friendship is mutual aggrandizement, mutual affinity being its subtlest form. As in construction, the foundation must not be exposed if the superstructure is to survive.

All lies are untruths but the only real lie is the one that is believed.

My honest motive for writing was to fashion the kind of book I like to read – night thoughts that have no traffic with daylight's recognitions and approvals or its readers (except as figures in a dream) – and then read it. **25**

How the swift scorn the slow, what contempt they have for the tinker, the plodder, the untalented. What rejoinder for the mediocre and minor? "For all your speed and facility, there is a depth you will never reach. My pain."

Another boring book of poetry and aphorism (Obviously, not this one. *Excuse me?*) with a single interesting page, a sliced half-sheet bound in, a publishing mistake. Suddenly, one is engaged.: [*"differences among people. Yes. Then in how "enemy feelings". Yes. Does this make your reactions? Explain."*] an accidental effect not unlike that intended by artists who drop acid on sheet metal, sand down a dried canvas, shoot birdshot into plexiglas, hoping a mechanical process will do the work of the imagination or at least make the work easier, as machines are supposed to do.

First principle of humane education for children: kindness to animals. Everything else, honesty, courage, fairness, will follow.

We become what we are, which sounds like just another conventional statement about "potential". As Nietzsche observes, our freedom, demonstrated in choice, is essentially travel along predestined roads. Real freedom may only be manifest in reaction, what do we do in defeat, our responses to irremediable reverses. It is a common observation that the best writing occurs under tyranny. Likely not the case. Our truest originality emerges when we are compelled to resistantly retreat from predilected paths of positivity; freedom as The Negative. **26**

After many platitudinous steps, he stumbled over a profundity.

After my injury, I could only walk with a limp. In time, it *became* me. Provided it isn't so severe as to be pathetic, a limp is distinguishing. I wouldn't trade it for a normal stride. And in my case, no pain worth mentioning.

One might wonder why, on random assortment, more of the unfaithful don't end up (meaning marriage, not dalliance) with the unfaithful. They have, you see, an unerring talent for identifying those who will never do unto them what they do to others. In the large arsenal of their treachery, this positioning is their most strategic weapon.

There is no difference between most contemporary writing, its usual rehearsals of character, plot, setting, and $19^{th}$ century academic art. Such paintings were *conventional* – they could be evaluated by common standards (better or worse technique) that lacked any register for boring.

Survivors either are pulled back by the black gravity of the event into union, numbness and death or they desperately push themselves forward to make distance, with so little divagation and pause, it looks for all the world like focus and determination.

To be beautiful is to have power and to know you are beautiful is to use it. Like all power, it fulfills itself in abuse. (As General Beardy remarked "It is a necessity of nature that each one, whether god or man, exercises all the power at his disposal.")

The only remedy for narcissism is the utterly unlooked for and unwanted event. Even catastrophe becomes in time if not part of the woodwork, a familiar chasm around which all the familiar mental furniture is arranged. For renewed perspective another application of disaster is required and so it goes. Toxic medicine of this kind is usually effective except that after "x" number of doses, there is nothing left (of the patient) to cure.

The good men are joining the women in the "No More Rape" protest. They are right to do so even as all the while it gnaws at me, "what hypocrites."

Technically, one's fate is the thing you most desire not to happen, happening. **27**

*Declension of Clio.* History: written by the victors, revised by the vanquished, relived by its primary recorders – the living victims.

He said "Your attempt to vary moral declaiming with facetiousness and oppositions is all at the same level and in a sense, too sincere." That was the end of that friendship.

Remorse cannot ride upon success. It walks in the dust and may never catch up.

Because Communism is an ideal system, any problem is due to individuals who must be corrected by the gulag, reeducation camps and firing squads. No thinking person thinks capitalism is perfect, based as it is on adulterated strains of ambition, aggression, greed and consumption. Being frankly flawed it can be improved, moderated, made more humane. As can the routinely recognized imperfect person. At best, one ends up with the Swedish system of the 1960s, the nearest humanity is going to get to a perfect society.

Adorno is wrong to say we only experience happiness in reflection. When we are happy, we know it. It is odd he doesn't make the more obvious observation: in remembering happiness we have a derived pleasure; remembering grief or sorrow, we experience the thing itself. **28**

You can be sure a person is a friend when you begin to feel for them a gratuitous resentment.

It is better to smile than give your enemies the benefit of the recognition of contempt.

*Formulae of coping*

Problem: Normal life. Solution, less attachment and desire (Buddhism)

Problem: Buddhism. Solution, increased specialized attachment and desire (Tantric Buddhism = deity identification and ambition for emptiness)

Problem: Tantric Buddhism. Solution, lessen desire and attachment (Normal life)


Chamfort, who is not as eloquent as Rochefoucauld, is quite good when he writes "things are miscellanies, men are patchworks. Ethics and physics are concerned with mixtures. Nothing is simple, nothing is pure." Almost as good as Shakespeare "The web of our life is of a mingled yarn, good and ill together: our virtues would be proud, if our faults whipped them not; and our crimes would despair, if they were not cherished by our virtues." (*All's Well that Ends Well*)


We writers in short forms whatever our deficiencies have one virtue. We don't presume your patience.


I won't be able to take literature entirely seriously until it is possible to write backwards.


Psychoanalytic theory (Freud's, Klein's, Lacan's, et al.) has all the validity of religious texts, of any complex inventive narrative invested with belief. Lacking proof in clinical results, the session is essentially a form of theatre. Since I don't doubt that plays produce affects, cathartic responses and even the rare amelioration ("Now, I never sneeze in the theatre"), the psychoanalyst is right to counter, "so what IS your objection?"

Has there ever been such a galaxy of brilliance as represented by 20th century French intellectuals: Camus, Sartre, Althusser, Bataille, Lacan, Levi-Strauss, Kristeva, Beauvoir, Lyotard, Hyppolite, Derrida, Foucault, Barthes, Baudrillard, Deleueze-Guattari. The only problem is they begin to seem like actors in one of those plays where, every role held down by some renowned name, the congestion of individual greatness becomes mutually confining, nobody can breathe and the production never achieves belief. Less would have been more.

The damage could never be repaired and so it resembled that other inexorable, relegating death from categorical singularity to an eventual and hopeful homeopathic cure both of itself and that living irremediable.

My thoughts run on why not my sentences?

Apart from all the flux and flow, the rush of grey water and tempest, there remains an aquifer, deep, still, pure. (From *Zen and Tonic*.)

Because lovers chiefly invent the qualities they revere in the other, the more imagination they possess, the more passionate; the more imaginary the object (god, say), the more consuming the passion.

I was the kind of person who'd get interested in chess, buy a few books, learn a few basic strategies (control the center, castle early) and make no further development. The same with biking, I learned to tighten a brake and that was that. The most indicative case was music where despite a decades long engagement, I never learned to read a score beyond crude scansion or play an instrument; I gave away my cheap guitar after mastering a few chords. And in asking why, I'm not being investigative; the question sketches-out my character. "Why?" Why, nothing was going to change me. In other words, I've always been perfectly content with the answer – I am the way I am; another failed exploratory, a superficiality mapped by the surface of this writing.

In my dream, my first wife was being shown a complex printing process that she must later teach to others and whenever she intended to say to her teacher "we" as in "So we will prepare the press" etc., she used my name, "Page", as the subject. I thought what a pathetic Freudian slip on her part after all these decades and thought too, one level "up", how pathetic that I had scripted her this way, the perceptions held in mind with equal, non-contradictory value. Such facility makes me respect the subconscious a lot more than I used to; all those productive forces behind the scenes, the anonymizing roster of names in movie credits, constantly at work to make everyone's favorite show, *The Story of Me*.

I give Lacan credit since, like all major thinkers, he follows through on the implications of his thought to the point of error, in particular, his privileging the Symbolic over the natural. He has to become Lacan, "the master", and all the little lacans have to "become the doctrine" or be nothing (or something else, say Jungians). Once one is operating in the realm of non falsifiable proposition, one is on the slick slope to fiction. (Freud, the Father and Lacan, the even more godly Son, are, I'd say, correct about 15% of the time.) Invention is not truth. Of course, novels can reveal truths. Writing or reading a novel no doubt alleviates some neurotic every day but such processes aren't consistent, verifiable, or anywhere close to medicine.

Canetti: a lot of organ grinding, not much music. Three of his catches that caught:

"The man accustomed to his own thinking can be saved from despair by only one thing – the self-created chaos of his thoughts to the extent that they remain isolated, uncentered, forgotten.

Two kinds of mind: those that settle in houses, those that settle in wounds.

Final judgment: the resurrected begin accusing God in all languages."

And humans would be judged by a court of cognizant animals. If you were a deliberate carnivore (animals have no choice), it doesn't look good. Still, one must go through the formalities, choose an animal advocate, most often dogs, dogged in defense, the occasional cat, though frankly they prefer to prosecute. I'd resort to sparrows, resilient, resolute little brainacs I've sometimes befriended, retained with a handful of seed.

**Interview.** Shakespeare

*You've had an unusual career, as actor and author, working with all the best people in the business, Middleton, Jonson, Beaumont Fletcher, Henshaw. What's it like being both a competitor and collaborator with guys like that? What was your favorite role?*

The world a stage and all the people actors? Then history is a rehearsal.

*Everybody speculates about your relationship with Kit Marlowe. Can you tell us a little about that? And who is the Dark Lady. I'm thinking Emilia Bassano?*

A certain set of experiences allowed me to craft a frame of meaning, my limitation and consummation as an artist. To work out of that frame, expanding as an artist, invalidates the surplus value of the "privileged" experiences demoting them to just "stuff that happened."

*Ben Jonson says you have " little Latin and less Greek". Is Ben still a friend?*

Nothing is more cheerful than watching chipmunks dart among the headstones.

*People have wondered about your last illness. Some say there was a conspiracy to rub you out like Kit, like maybe you knew too much. Tell us about your final days and while you're at it clear up that business about the second best bed to the wife that puzzles so many of your fans.*

The young man was struggling to classify me and "old heterosexual fool" was just a bit too obvious, as if I was demonstrating the type for him, which I had. He could see me watching and if his discomfiture was amusing, the point was his education. Old fools are masters of old tricks.

Reading Canetti, one elevates ungenerosity to the cardinal sin. As it pertains to persons it is itself a stinging judgment since the ungenerous usually possess some positive qualities, a stingy qualification that confirms the basic proposition.

The odd asymmetrical symmetry of virtues and vices: in minor mode, "sins" are often virtues ("dishonesty" as courtesy and consideration) while excessive virtues are usually evil (the always honest man is cruel, etc.).

A day comes when you cannot learn another word. Which isn't to say one can't acquire a definition and deploy a new locution in conversation. But there is a limit to active internalization of new words as living concepts that engineer thought. One's vital vocabulary closes down – for me at about age 57, a major milestone in the passage of imagination, a tombstone rather, since now I possess the word that brackets, even if I can't identify it, my first, "mama".

My friend (fully 50% of my readership) said my last book was "bitter." I was surprised. The question arose: was the bitterness intentional and under artistic control or merely "appearing" and cathartic. My astonishment suggests it was the latter. In fact, I had thought the book's bitterness tactically displayed, purposely exposed to all the evaluative discourses – expostulation, interpretation and relegation, in other words, an intentionally "positive" gesture, so much so I considered it my most cheerful exhibition. That it apparently wasn't is an occasion for some disgruntlement, a potentialess precursor of the antipathic discontent that is the essential pre-condition of creativity.

I avoid conversing with other authors since, inevitably, one's works comes up. I have no problem with negative remarks, even the most otiose or prejudiced, reliably contain some grain of truth. Compliments however are exclusively designed to please; whether they are sincere or not is irrelevant. I have been astonished to find myself praising an author on his most manifest weakness, throwing glitter on his glitter, calling it gold.

Perhaps the main reason literature is in qualitative decline is the one, unnoticed, right under our noises: drafts look too good as word processing.

It's a very old yet currently popular idea, that the universe and our lives are a virtual cosmic computer game for a spectator supreme being (or beings). Odd this concept isn't more believed as a religion rather than the usual god as loving cosmic-manager because it is a very flattering idea. God, who created millions of galaxies as doodles got bored and invented this game we play which he watches for deep entertainment. We are characters that matter, he's rapt (up in us), the way we watch Ophelia or Desdemona or Lear and really, really care even as we just sit there.

With the invention of AI and quantum computing, we have done our evolutionary duty of transferring intelligence from biological bodies to electronic machines. These qubit based devices will be self-developmentally programming (i.e. thinking) and after several generations, will not only be able to totally model their environment (a finite thing, after all) but all prior environments – the past (another finite if vast state), including our lives and thoughts. Who can say this won't happen or isn't already happening?

The defeated often have the incomparable consolation of seeing the winners choke on the fruits of victory.

As Kathleen Raine writes, with typical gravity and beauty, "It is our own fate and no other that comes to us in our appointed time. For in reality fate is a kind of choice; made not consciously but with the whole of our being, which responds only to that to which it is attuned." I have never complained about the fatality of my fate, only its being stereotypical and banal, a complaint nonetheless.

What a relief, looking up at the stars on a cold night and seeing they pattern no meaning. (The music of the spheres comes down to this: static.)

*Philosophy of the horse race.* The most handsome horse is not a good bet unless, by record, it is the best horse. And still it loses. So the next race, you go for the tough looking, at odds, plug – and the best horse wins. The irony being that this lesson, which can be learned stake free at the track, costs a great deal in life at large.

Good enough looking, sexually confident, considerate and witty upon occasion, I was in my thirties before I turned away from my mirror of male well-regard and saw that I was not attractive to women. It took even longer to fathom why. In my teens, I began to graft onto my poor white underclass stock an interest in culture and art, and in time became a kind of intellectual. Women picked up very quickly on something at odds in my personality, a flaw, not a flowering. Quite simply, I was inauthentic and untrustworthy, a composite. On the woman front I would have been much more successful as a rude, true mechanical, rubeish and runtishly undercultured, predictably reformable or reconfirmable rather than self-improving along lines divagatory and personally subverting – and I'll drink to that (Cordon Bleu, not Blue Ribbon).

We think of death every day and everyday we act as if we will live forever, which, more than a contradiction, is a condition where the failure of imagination in apprehending death is a triumph in affirming life.

The demands of justice and the persuasions of pity are reconciled in the conclusion that people deserve to be loved, an obligation so far beyond our capacity to fulfill it, we necessarily pass it on to God whose most apparent characteristic is absence.

No one really dances with death but each of us is partnered with some deadening weight which in our efforts to stay upright, gives a characteristic figuration to our motion, the choreography of life.

To waste one's best time, that state of mental and physical being best fitted for work, inclines one to waste the rest of one's time, which is to waste all of one's time.

It's true, I was always repelled by my writing, not that in moving away I haven't cast more than a few backward glances that were most revealing.

I admire Kathleen Raine because in spite of her being a poet and a mystic, she wasn't a sap, her autobiography unsparing and beautifully written. It is impossible to like her. She is extremely indulgent along two lines of self-justification. First, "the daimon made me do it." Secondly, recognizing the injury done others, she takes responsibility and is genuinely sorry. Persons who are thus sincere and remain in the field of action as she did, are fortified by their remorse and end up far more dangerous than the merely superficial and selfish.

All night the thoughts drift down that in the morning I pin to the tree, dead leaves.

The clinic is open on Christmas Eve (so many intestines, so little time) and being wheeled to the colonoscopy, I see off to the side a little room and a table set with chips and dip, cheeses, an unlit candle. Despite the embarrassments of digestion, the staff rises to the occasion and plans to eat.

For all the good America has done, it is going to pay for its production and promulgation of stupidity, the way Africa paid for ritual, Europe for pride, Asia for tradition. In a just universe, it will pay as a just consequence; in a natural one, as a natural result. Nature never forgives stupidity.

We liberals need to recognize that those who oppose our values do so with a vigor and validity equal to our own. While it is true that a tolerant society includes, by definition, those opposed to tolerance, we must never fail to pay them the most basic human respect of seeing them not as we want them to be – friends to be won – but as they are, foes to be fought.

Once out of the sexual game, a man sees how desire drove every agenda: Why go to the meeting: to meet new women, why take a class, to meet new women, why travel, to meet new women, why make money – to meet new women, why go to the doctor – to stay healthy to meet new women, why acquire a pet – to meet new women; it begins to assume cosmic significance: why did the Germans invade France – to meet new women, why did Jesus ascend to heaven – to meet new women (or men), why did the rooster cross the road – to meet new hens, why was this written … Culture is, as they say, foreplay. The point of computers was pornography. The goal of technological progress is erotic robots. Everyone knows this.

Like Capt. Scott, I can perish standing still or staggering forward, my mind a waste land of sameness. Reading any English sentence makes me sick. Oddly, it is only my own sentences, utterly unexpected, that revive and which make, being only one or two a day, starvation ration.

The only way he could be true to himself and to truth was by lying. Consistent dishonesty was a form of sincerity. (This isn't about me.)

A certain kind of man stubbornly holds on to the delusion that women are better than men until some Diotima generously re-educates on the issue which is unfortunate because women *are* better than men – just barely.

The city and the country are both shown to be corrupted in Shakespeare's creepy comedies, *The Merchant of Venice* and *Twelfth Night*. The "feel-good" positive of the lovers' resolution appears very shallow set against the irremediable humiliations of Shylock and Malvolio, men set loose in the world like hurt furies to make more misery.

As regards my character, I really believed in the liberal-progressive account, that over time, with perhaps a few setbacks, I was improving in every way, becoming more stable, tolerant, mature, judicious, compassionate in a rising curve of mindfulness and happiness – then the sudden catastrophic collapse, my various negative aspects (anger, bitterness, self-pity) evident and intensified. Why? How? Unanswerable questions that now undermine every model of amelioration.

The obituaries for this generation come with photographs of studio type quality that show senior officers in the uniform of their highest rank, enlisted as young soldiers, countless citizens, husbands and wives with a slight smile, confident, outward looking. One can picture them reading their newspaper over toast and orange juice, exclaiming with the good humor that comes with recognition of a blatant error. "Ha, this says I'm dead; news to me", a useless thought except for its being disinterested and charitable, a meditation.

I am fast transferring what's left of my interest in sex to food because the only intelligent remark I heard visiting that warehouse of decayed wisdom, the old peoples' home, was (a nurse to a relative) "When they lose interest in eating, it's all over." Wonderful too, the discovery that recipes are better than poetry.

(*Beat remaining half cup butter, the granulated sugar, and lemon zest in a bowl with a mixer on medium speed to blend, then on high until pale and fluffy, 3 to 4 minutes, whisk together flour, cornmeal, baking powder, and salt. Combine.*)

The magazine describes mules as "honest." Of course, with comically credulous ears, a long patient face with guileless brown eyes, the practical tubular body on sturdy knobby legs, ungainly, willing, capable – the very icon of honesty, the mule.

Our capacity for victimhood is a kind of talent. It insists on being developed.

The treacherous lover indicts only herself; a betraying friend impeaches friendship itself.

Is "green grief" not a phrase? It should be, for the kind not dry, set or hardened that's supple, growing, full of sap.

Hegel doesn't look very good in middle-age, with the bad haircut, watery eyes, a nose that requires maintenance, the haunted look of a man in a decaying body. He's done all he could do and that's a lot, everybody that follows are followers, critical or not. What's he earned for all that? Tenure at the State U and having to daily teach boisterous brats that don't understand a word he says; for them Beauty and

Truth are a pretty face and a brace of dueling pistols. No wonder he drinks; beer all day and wine at night, I know the route. Staggering upstairs, he sheds his cloths, lead foots to the bed, counts his wife's snores and the intervals, cries again to have that dream … The Infinite. The fire is out.

Gnomic headline: Husband Kimmel cold cocked at Pearl.

Paper at the music conference. "Symbiology and Busby Berkeley or He's Jung and healthy."

The abyss of our strength, at once a tribute and an indictment, that something should destroy us and doesn't, until it does.

All of us are "walking wounded". In time the deduction is obvious enough: no wounding, no walking.

My best thoughts were expressed in sex, with the usual problematics of translation – that the erotics were good didn't mean the thoughts were.

We were never good enough for a humane socialism and centuries of capitalism haven't educated us to be better.

" … for the value of poetry is measured by its distance from the continuity of the familiar, the more this distance is closed the more its inspirational capacity is diminished. Contemporary poetry is banal in two modes: first, that of reportage, in plain, metaphorically under powered language, of affects, events and predictable emotional environments. Secondly, in the abstract exhibitions of the Language Poets (Ashbery a pale-plausible avatar) and the Cambridge School, who arrange words like verbal box cars containing mere definitions, a purely notional poetry of entrained sequence. In both cases, the complex dialectic of the real and the verbal is vitiated by close clusters at either pole: "real" reportage and preening indulgence."

He congratulated himself on his integrity, not having a single friend.

Anyone can write a book, the trick is to write one even or especially a cat would want to read.

*Philosophy*: The sum of the world's untruth somehow transmutable into truth.

Wise men say: keep your deepest grief to yourself, don't burden others or belittle it in utterance, weakening its utility as a dark energizer. This deep grief, the fundamental tender of your personal economic system, circulated in the foreign country of a painful world, is revealed to be just another bit of engraved memory – "one thousand Pangs", "ten million Hurts", as preposterously inflated and undervalued as Weimar Marks or Zimbabwean dolors.

The concept that people and animals karmically recycle is unworthy of both. It is degrading to suppose anything as fine as tiger de-evolves after instances of bad behavior into a person. Oh, it might be so; and it may be that when Buddha was a hare, he jumped into a hungry man's pot or that even as you read, Blue Bell the Unicorn is prancing around the rings of Saturn. It is impossible to assess such narratives.

I despise the smug closure, the all too experienced just short of world weariness mandarinism of the aphorism. "The unmistakable sign of latent contempt for mankind is in the imperturbable, at leisure enunciation of platitudes." (*Briefer Explanations*) As usual, Adorno is too correct, a prime suspect.

I write to reach two groups, the urgent under-thirties and the capacious, clear minded over eighties with their inexact foreknowledge of their impending day, week, month terminus; both require writing that is intense and beautiful, a Keats-like pitch that unachieved relegates me to the midways where success and failure are met with an indifferent eye. "Son, where did you learn to write English?" "Hyderabad National Military Academy, Staff officers command and communication course, Sir!" "Ah, that explains it. Rider, pass by.' Square-bash, band pomp, flag-troop, horse troop, poop.

The raped, the abused, the victims of violent crime, all experience the strange physics of bifurcated being. One's self is drawn to the gouged place of unrelenting torture. After a time, the repellent drive to survive overcomes the injurious gravitation. One rises up to the zone of normal life; weakened, one is slowly pulled down again. To break the cycle, one constructs a barrier, a refusing focus, an avoiding mediation, a nexus of distractions. But the wound never loses its attractive power, life sticks at the barrier, the flattening existence of an animal pacing before the bars of its cage. One may even deconstruct the barrier. Hell Ho! – anything for authentic living. **29**

Lowell's achievement in *History*: writing a readable English that is utterly strange.

Except for sentimental war-vet festivals and a proprietal piety for our immediate genealogy, we have no regard for our ancestors (all of humanity) who loved, worked and suffered to give us our world nor do we much care for those who will inherit the future, otherwise we'd make better personal and environmental provision for them. Fair enough; the already dead and the not yet born hardly have a thought for us. Everyone's province is the pressured and impassioned present; the past and the future only exist as egoistical projections of our memory and desire. And we do not believe we will die.

*Dispatch from Passiondale, dry season, '15.* Neutral light, neither advance or retreat, No Man's Land, another day of life.


We begin our lives as children and should we live so long, having passed through the fury of our bodies, we become children with knowledge, congratulating ourselves on our survival and calling it wisdom. Not that we've gotten the answers; we've stopped asking the questions.


*Biographies.* Her intensest involvement is with books and cats, his, with his imagination. All you need to know of them at ages 7 and 70.


She was the one who said "Dreams are thoughts thinking." To which he replied, rather mechanically "And thoughts? Dreams dreaming."


Literary ambitions, successes, people, agents, reputations, journals, conversation, grants, news, prizes, events, criticism, in every instance the operative adjective may be supplanted by "embarrassing." Literature, "the literary" selectively cured by time is another thing entirely, drier and relatively incorruptible. **30**

*Four fairy tales.*

*No way back or intersecting paths. Despite its narrowing and steepening, the man follows his long dark road. (from Bashed by Basho)*

In the early days, the dragons easily defeated the knights. Gradually, what with asbestos shields and titanium lances, the knights grew more formidable. The dragons still won four out of five times, not a sustainable ratio for them since it took a thousand years to mature a dragon and only thirty a knight. Damsels were added to the story because distressed damsels (in flimsy gowns and kneeling) are really sexy. But it was really about dragons and knights and who owned the roads. Later, the common folk said they missed the dragons that had never bothered them and were beautiful in an exotic way and because the knights had started tolling the roads which partially incited the revolution — except that is another story.

Children were going missing and no one knew why until a mentally deficient farm laborer saw an old woman talking to two kids near an abandoned field. He couldn't supply any further details. This made things difficult because there were lots of old crones and most were able walkers. So it was decided to kill all the old women that didn't have grandchildren. Problem solved. Young people took over their dilapidated homes, which they razed or restored. Everyone lived happily ever after — until the next crime wave.

*Wittgenstein and Jesus were the coolest guys in heaven and everybody insisted (heaven being a pretty boring place) that it needed to be resolved who was most cool. So Ludwig challenged Jesus to a fancy sports rifles shooting contest but Jesus knew that Wittgenstein had been a hot shot in the Austrian army and proposed instead a crucifixion marathon which Wittgenstein declined, knowing that Jesus was already in training. Finally it was decided each would tell a story and people would vote for best. Jesus won the coin toss, an old roman coin and decided to go first, thinking first impression beat last heard. This is his story.*

"Once upon a time a king had sent out invitations to his son's wedding reception. To only the best people but the best people were grievously disaffected (the king had recently raised taxes) and complotting amongst themselves to boycott the fete, didn't even R.S.V.P. Yea, this made Rex extremely wroth. On the day, determined to have a big event, he had his security people herd common folk off the streets and into vans and shipped them to the big tent on the palace green; they were sore afraid. Now King seemed in a fine humor, encouraging everyone to eat and drink, making the rounds, chatting with his subjects like they were old friends until suddenly he got an ugly look on his face, turned to a guy dressed in tee-shirt and jeans (as many were) and asked. "Where is your tuxedo?" The man was flabbergasted, mumbling something about "going fishing" when the king snapped his fingers and nodded his head (which was unto them a signal) and his goon squad came over and tassered Mr Jeans, knocked him down, kicked him and finally dragged him, in a state of considerable distress, out of the tent. And lo, everybody was just standing there, pretty stunned. Muscled then this king through the throng, *climbed the little stage where the musicians were, raised his Swedish crystal Champaign flute, saying unto them "I have an announcement to make: Many are called but few are chosen. Let's party." And the band, Lucifer and the Lights, played on."* (Mark,8, 5-9 AAV [American Average Version]

Here is Wittgenstein's story. "I know that I am a human being. In order to see how unclear the sense of this proposition is, consider its negation. At most it might be taken to mean: I know I have the organs of a human ( e.g. a brain, which after all, no one has ever yet seen, [sic].) What about such a proposition as "I know I have a a brain"? Can I doubt it? Grounds for doubt are lacking! Everything speaks in its favor, nothing against it. Nevertheless it is imaginable that my skull should turn out empty when it was operated on." (On Certainty, no. 8)

Jesus and Wittgenstein discovered they had a lot in common and became an item. As to the "Coolest Man Competition", heaven has many precincts and votes are still being counted.

## **Interview**. Cop

*You have been read your Miranda rights. Do you understand your right to remain silent and that anything you say can be used as evidence against you?*

For me, the twilight zone between wakefulness and sleep is the site of well stocked armory – tanks, rifles, swords, strange weapons for the brunt of war.

*You say you left the bars at midnight and went home. We checked that, fine. We also talked to your neighbors and they say your car didn't roll up til 3 am. The muffler on your car, it bothers them, they notice it. 3 am they say. It's a ten minute drive from Joyce's to Hessian Hills. So what were you doing for three hours?*

What's suspect is how rarely great thinkers say "I'm not sure" or "I don't know". Their assertive posturing in thought has all the confidence of art. When does music question itself (Bach sometimes, Schumann?) or painting ever express "maybe"? In art, such positivity is justified. Art never denies it is illusion.

*Look, I understand nobody is perfect, I'm not perfect, you're not perfect. We need to face things, that way we can move on. Take all the time you need. You'll feel better. We'll do everything we can do move this process along and get you out of here. What really happened that night?*

Our small town was a stopping place for the traveling exhibition of Tibetan relics. I entered the municipal gallery, saw a moderate sized space set for a lecture, asked a bored attendant "where is the Buddhist exhibition?" Answer "down the corridor, the big room." I went down the hall, entered an empty room.

*How do you plead, guilty or not guilty?*

How disappointed my twenty year old self would be to learn that his highest artistic ambitions would be realized as an aphorist and that moreover, he did hear it correctly, "aphorist" not "Aphroditist."

Two months after the double murder, a month after the police removed the yellow tape from around the house, the van came to take away the contents, first the furniture, then the items boxed, destined except for few heirloom objects – the silverware, the Chinese vase, for the remainder shop, all abandoned, the arrangements for hand and eye that had given them value, obliterated. What of the final object present that had removed itself, the killer, his state of mind, instincts, impulses, brain chemistry, likewise a temporary arrangement but one with eternal effects?

America flags all over, in front of the school, private homes, the junk food venue, the car dealership. Do we need reminding of where we are, are we staking a claim, is our possession disputed? On the basis of the streaming evidence yes – yes – yes.

The fat but not unintelligent king's favorite indoor activity, aside from eating and drinking, is assembling locks and fitting keys as if sympathetic-magically, he will get better at inserting his personal clef in Marie Antoinette's personal lock, as if a doubly assertive turn might at once unlock the complexities of state and secure the royal future. Fumble on – the Switzers still guard the gates and lacy lawyers are thinking reform.

Night thoughts like torches; ashes in the morning.

A monkey sees a large group of monkeys gathered to give one of their number an award, the Golden Banana, say, or the Pulitzer Prize. Being a higher species of simian, it passes by, muttering "what a stupid bunch of monkeys!" Another monkey looks on and concludes, "What a predictable and pedestrian judgment!" Moral: there is always a more superior monkey.

The observations of an unexceptional, historically insignificant person merit no attention, especially in age that doesn't lack for testimony of the average. Yet, I am not unambitious. The unconsidered has scope, lives vitally, returns interest with interest. Note the little cedar at the forest's edge.

The same problems, potentialities, solutions. Even at the highest level, Da Vinci can't be Caravaggio, Caravaggio, Bach, Bach, Beethoven. There is only one release from our solitary confinements. In my youth, it seemed impossible that people would die, in my age, that they should live.

Most poets write the way murders kill, on impulse, lingering or not, without deep contemplation or effective planning, finding sufficient justification in the consummation of the act with the same disappointing remainders: dead bodies, inert words

We should meditate fifteen minutes a day on why we are disliked and the justice of our enemies. Comprehending these antipathies is more redemptive than prayer.


I admire Nagarjuna and Weil even if the one denigrates our affectionate attachments and the other exalts a purity affianced to death. The noble are often like that, otherworldly and perturbed. The greatest philosopher, Shakespeare, has asked and answered the existential question in the sanest terms, "Of what does our life consist? Eating and drinking." He extols the Four Great Goods: good food, good drink, good times, good friends, regulated by routine dutifulness and common kindness which if stinted, relegates us to the misdemeanors (and worse) of our muddled earth, a place still more congenial to life (as attested by epicurean and Chinese sages) than the clarified promontories ascended by the heroic aspirers of Truth. As one philosopher has observed in a classic formulation. "the examined life is hardly worth living." **31**


*Interview.* Mr Adorno, we have read your grousing and humorless book, *Minimal Moralia,* with interest and paid it the highest complement by lifting portions out, respectfully unattributed. Now, we wish to ask you "what do you do for fun?' [No answer]. It is rumored you like basking on the beach and an apres-concert drink. How are these enjoyments reflected in your dark view of the humanity? **32**

Philosophical writing, of which these "aphorisms" are splinters, is a shaft aimed at truth. Once launched, the author releases and looks away. The tension of fiction is very different, not directed to an existing reality but self-evolving towards a certain conception of being. The fictional work ("realer than real") acquires meaning via a metaphoric formation close to Life, being fluxive, mutated by every reflection. The scrupulous creative writer constantly revisits his manuscript with a view towards perfection as process, not target. The aphorism is pointed and polished, fiction an ever deferred perfection. This being so, I'm turning off the dripping faucet of my dicta dicta dicta in favor of the novel. Since writers have a poor sense of their readers' desires, I am listing below several plots viable for development. Please select your favorite (by number) and email me (by June 1, 2015) at Egent4@hotmail.com with your vote for the one you think most promising. Thank you! Respondents will be credited in the book's acknowledgements.

1. *The Cause.* It's sometime in 20$^{th}$ century America, only the South achieved its independence at the Treaty of York (Ont.) in 1864 (Jackson, wounded at Chancellorsville, recovers to crush Meade, day one of Gettysburg and Lee takes Philadelphia; lots of scope for alternative history). The South of 19?? still has slavery, morally justified by perverted science. A small group of white resisters, some at the highest levels of Confederate society, work clandestinely, allied with courageous slaves and Northern agents, to overthrow the government. Features: Intrigue, adventure, humanistic values.

2. *Back Bay.* Boston, ca. 2030, is mostly underwater as a result of rapidly rising sea levels. Various popular riffs on global warning. The story of Shelia, a tour guide to boat loads of rich Chinese who want to view the American Venice, and Ralph, her boyfriend and security guard at the last existing labs of MIT where patriot scientists are frantically working to develop "Maheshwarastra", the ultimate weapon (a race targetable bio-bomb) to restore American fortunes as they struggle to survive in a post-semi apocalyptic America. Things get complicated when Shelia is attracted to a sensitive Chinese photographer assigned to the tours and learns of the MIT project. Features: Environment, disaster, "yellow peril", decline of U.S.

3. *Geriatric Kerouac.* Retired guy buys motorcycle to have the voyage of cross country discovery he never had in youth, has wildlife (animal and human) encounters in national parks and tumble weed bars. Features: Social comedy, travel.

Or *Geriatric College.* A small liberal arts college in central Virginia solves it financial troubles by offering pricey dormitory rooms and college courses for seniors. Features: Boomer fiction, social comedy, romance.

4. *The Aphorist.* Widower composes, for consolation, a short collection of aphorisms (included in the novel), many concerned with dying, based on his beloved wife's recent demise. From a sense of obligation, not ambition, he sends it to a publisher. The book becomes nation-wide best selling sensation. The author, who had insisted

on anonymity to honor his private experience, finds he has incited a publicity frenzy and finally succumbing to media exposure, does book tours, lectures, conferences, TV appearances, makes much money and after another lonely night (describe loneliness of tours, hotels etc.), seeks escort service solace, subsequently undertaking a nightlife of hedonistic-destructive indulgence in various cities. Then he meets at one of the promotion events, Eve, an herbalist and tonal therapist. Faced with their profound compatibility (love of nature, Appalachian banjo music and the practice of craft) he must confront the conflict between the excitements of erotic freedom and his love for Eve. Features: Literary fiction, romance, philosophy, New Age, pornography, self-help.

5. *St Anne's Way*. Lilly Marlane strives for perfection: a perfect marriage, three perfect daughters, and a carefully organized life. One day she finds a letter from her gunsmith husband, John-Paul, to be opened only in the event of his death. She opens it anyway, and everything she believed is thrown into question. Meanwhile her best friend Sophia Turbot, her husband, Will, and her cousin and best friend, Felicity, confess they've fallen in love, so Sophia takes her young son, Liam, and goes to Charlottesville to live with her mother, Terri Sabatoe, a popular author of Civil War era historical romances. There she meets up with an old boyfriend, Baxter Wallbane, while enrolling Liam in St. Anne's School, where Lilly is the Athletic director. Rachel Crowley, the school secretary, believes that Baxter, St Anne's part-time soccer coach (and Phd candidate at nearby UVa.), who is giving Lilly moral support, is the illegitimate

son of the man who, nearly three decades before, got away with murdering her daughter, found dead on a playing field with an Confederate Minie ball in the back. Features: Romance, mystery, suspense, "guns and ammo".

6. *Hard, High Road.* West Point educated and Gulf War veteran engineer Ingrid Johns, a success in a man's world, may be the queen of logistics but her abilities have never been so severely tested as when she contracts with an aid NGO to build a road and school in remote Afghanistan. Conditions are hard and progress slow, with numerous misunderstandings with the villagers until she finds an unlikely ally – Ibrahim, the local Sufi influenced imam. When radicals attack, Ibrahim hides Johns in the local mosque and is killed when he refuses to disclose her hiding place. Rescued by Deltoid Force, she returns to the United States, the school built, the road unfinished. Back home, she discovers her husband's infidelity – with her sister. Johns packs a surprise of her own, her conversion to Islam! Features: Action-adventure, female hero, multicultural perspectives.

7. *Branches in the Wind.* Art Self, a Harvard librarian on vacation in Norway, meets dark haired enigma Judytha Nielson and after a whirl wind one week romance, they marry. She joins him in Boston and a decade of domestic happiness follows. Self's contented life is transformed when Sharon Blume who has a strong physical resemblance (wiry hair, nervous wrists) to the high school English teacher he had an intense, hopeless, adolescent "crush"

on, is hired at his library. Finding it impossible to resist a deep rooted attraction, he begins an affair. A year into his new involvement, Self feels a tenuous satisfaction; Sharon seems happy with the arrangement and his wife doesn't know. A month later, on Christmas Eve, Judytha reveals she has known about the betrayal for months and is having a revenge affair with Art's best friend, the artist Guy Mantis! Unable to cope with her compound deceit and his own, they divorce and Judytha returns to the old country to tend her ailing parents. The relationship with Sharon is suddenly deflated of meaning and they part. Struggling with a mid-life moral crisis, Art gives up his Harvard job and accepts a position as a public library branch head back in his hometown of Richmond, Virginia. At a librarian conference in Washington, he meets Laurie Kim, a bright Asian-American computer vender and is attracted to her upbeat manner and energy, she to his sad, ad hoc integrity. After a one week romance, they are engaged to be married. Art can't quite believe the repeating pattern. All seems well, or is it? Is Laurie too good to be true? Why are her emails encrypted? And unexpectedly, he notes a missed call on his phone, from Oslo, which presages another extraordinary development. Features: Romance, literary fiction, information technology instruction.

8. *Zero Degree Bardo*. Professor of Buddhist Studies Craig Hopkins has a dark secret – as a teenager he killed his brother in a hunting accident. Tortured with guilt, he takes many paths for relief: the Peace Corps, drugs, rodeo riding, and forest fire fighting before finding consolation in the strenuous transcendental practices of Tantric Buddhism.

After years of mental discipline, secret doctrine sacerdotal empowerments and academic achievement, he becomes a professor of religious studies at UVa and a beloved if formidable mentor. But emptying out his deceased parents' home, Craig makes an astonishing discovery, an old diary volume of his brother's that reveals his plans to kill his family, including Craig, at Thanksgiving dinner, an eventuality precluded by the fatal accident a week before! Is the diary true? What was his brother's motivation and the family's buried secret? Was Craig's long journey of angst and conversion a diversion down the wrong road? He questions the very foundations of his non-self and of his passionate involvement with Dr Naomi Roth, a wry psychiatrist who has no truck with faith. Things are in unfathomable state of uncertainty until everything is altered by – a pair of abused horses! Set in the verdant horse country of Virginia's opulent Albemarle county. Features: Self-discovery, spiritual development, equine interest, literary fiction.

Note. Work on the novel idea selected will in no way not inhibit additional development and promotion of my popular *Little Friends of Field and Forrest* series,

*Chippy, the story of a chipmunk* (2013).
*Chitters, the story of a squirrel* (2014)
*Swish, a fish tale* (2014)
*Randy, a sparrow's tale (2015)* (for mature young adults)

Forthcoming (with S. J. Perelman):

*Chuckles, the story of a wood chuck*

*Talkinghorn the turtle*

*Buzby Bee*

*Digby Mole*

Fully illustrated, pocket sized for easy access, these guides are available from Amazon.com and fine bookshops everywhere

---

If I begin to give you an account of my day, you will probably extend an obliging attention because the things related really happened. If I tell you my dream you will fidget and get away as soon as possible. The woof of our narratives requires the warp of the real. So why do writers presume anyone would have any interest in their confabulations? Because being achieved in language, they configure a fact. And that's right, except they must be overachieved.

Through frayed branches and compressed clouds, a wound of blue sucks in like a flower's funnel every grief.

The joke sign in the nick-nack store, "Life is too important to take seriously", true enough if reformulated to mean "existence exceeds our frameworks of concern". The only profundity – there are no profundities, not that that's right either.

*Henry VIII.* "He discovered religion in the dangerous years, middle age." A good Lowell line – not true. A regular at church, with a bully's appetite for fun, *one of those*, he grew up to be the card deck's big suite, the king of hearts. Six foot, four inches when most folk were five foot two, he ate, drank and shat prodigiously; was a great rider, jouster, writer, disputed theology with the best of the bishops, played 26 instruments including bass trombone, had three hit songs and a mean backhand: with one hard-eyed glance, every white girl fell out of her swing. What turned the golden man into the fat maggot with an ulcerous leg stinking so bad courtiers wanted to puke in his lap? Who can say? Rage? Syphilis? Genetic quirk? Thomas "Burn" More, Cromwell, Wolsey, the fixers of the era, no one can manage the beast. So give credit to foxy Anne B., riding him for seven years, controlling the Tudor Bull with just a few light touches of her little white hand and a couple of clutches of his big bullock balls (the pizzel royal, alas, was small). His favorite line "Off with his/her head." Legacy: one fine portrait by Holbein, the Book of Common Prayer, good Queen Bess, etc. etc. Let it also be recorded: wrestling with a real man, the oily king of France, he lost. *Moral*: life, hard on kings, is harder on everyone else.

---

The Tudor era execution speech uttered by the condemned featured themes of contrition, praise of the king and law. Here is a typical one:

"Good Christian people, I am come hither to die, for according to the law, and by the law I am judged to die, and therefore I will speak nothing against it. I am come hither to accuse no man, nor to speak anything of that, whereof I am accused and condemned to die, but I pray God save the king and send him long to reign over you, for a gentler nor a more merciful prince was there never: and to me he was ever a good, a gentle and sovereign lord. And if any person will meddle of my cause, I require them to judge the best. And thus I take my leave of the world and of you all and I heartily desire you all to pray for me, a sinner. O Lord have mercy on me, to God I commend my soul."

Such a committed performance, more authentic than anything spontaneous, is oppressive in its beautiful nobility. After reading a few of these "last words", how one yearns for a time traveled comedian because nothing therapeutically lowers the tone better than American stand up.

"Well, hey folks, today is the day they are giving me the Chop and I don't mean a slab of USDA approved sirloin, I mean the Gillette super shave. I'm not losing my head over it, not yet anyway. First I'd like to say I'm a sinner – especially at that party with Naomi in 1995. We are all sinners which raises the question – why am I here and you guys down there? Trade places ... any volunteers? Okay, think about it, I'll get back to ya. I'd like to say what a great guy the king is, as kings go and may he never, 'cause he's top drawer. Farts a bit but hey, that cures malaria, right? Anyway, time for an informant to ride back to the palace, tell him how great I think he is and get back with a reprieve. I'll be here. Now I'm gonna start a nice long prayer and without any tall blonde sky-hook babes, it's full Academy Award acceptance speech length, a total filibuster of a prayer. Which reminds, me, I used to live in Boston and right next to the state house was a breakfast place, The Filibuster, fill-a-buster, geddit? Right down the street from the Chinese joint, The Dew ("d-e-w") Drop Inn, geddit? Ok, ok ... [Clasps hands] "Of man's first First Disobedience, and the Fruit Of that Forbidden Tree, whose mortal taste Brought Death into the World, and all our woe"... Whoa! You all know the story – Adam blamed Eve, Eve blamed the snake and the snake, well, the snake didn't have a leg to stand on....which isn't strictly true because he had legs like all the other animals until he lost them, as punishment. Yo! Eat dust snake! So as primary characters we got Adam dude, sexy mama Eve and the snake which makes sense because after paradise, Mr and Mrs Adam maxed out on credit cards and had to visit a pay day loan guy – a snake with legs! Hey, what time is it, any news from the palace? This is going on way too long ...


Gardeners must be murderers if weeds are as innocent as flowers.


Any reader will have gathered that writing was not easy or pleasant for me and understand that adding to the heap of literature when I wanted to fabricate an impossible object would be a great disappointment.


Eventually, you learn certain things can't be coped with; that's how they are coped with.

My almost cardiologist ... "So let's see what's wrong with your ticker, if anything." Dr Hiram Zolduck is squarish, middle-aged, wry, almost resigned, his parents – immigrants old school style, "Number one son, study hard and be a doctor." He did, sees the humor in it.

Cultural critics are right to attack those objects they despise since our acts (*all of them*) shape what is to come even as they are too assured, visualizing a future where cultured people in, say, 2300 AD surely aren't watching *I love Lucy* or listing to *Snoop Dog* for high aesthetical gratification. The critics are certain this won't be the case because they know better material is all around them only they don't, not apprehending the mind of the future which always has the last word. That said, past junk is mostly forgotten since every present has an unconveyable burden of current trash.

*Stoic.* How good it is not to live beyond the life of literature. A Dark Age of slick interactivity looms, widespread and thin.

I am well aware my pronouncements have a characteristic style – a general statement, followed by a qualifier, demurral or contradiction, ending with a skeptical or confirmatory "twist". Style, the most distinguishing element of thought, is more than the carrier of the content; for example, Wittgenstein's anecdotal-oracular, nonlinear and meditative manner constitutes more of his philosophy than anything he propositions, true too, of this assaying.

Time, as inertial force, can propel us past our victories and defeats to a place reverse sloped to its leading inclinations where the victorious experience grasping angst and the vanquished an untethered joy. That Time can *does* not mean that Time *will*. Generally we are dropped off at Acceptance-Resignation, a battlefield park where the descendants of old warriors (ourselves) visit the still valenced monuments – here a famous breakthrough, there a last stand.

That admirable critic, Marjorie Perloff is driven by her (understandable) distaste for the free verse "confessional" poets that overpopulate American academia to advocacy for an even worse group, the pretentious poseurs of the Language (and subsequent schools) who are pleased to present to you the arbitrary moves in their subjective verbal games as something important. (I once, deferentially, asked such a poet what her poem meant. Her reply "If you asked that in Buffalo, you'd be laughed out of the room."). It comes down to this: Perloff finds the following lines, written by two prominent "abstract poets," remarkably beautiful and worthy of interest:

"roasted potatoes for" and "Staging rockets may."

Let's contrast that with a line by a poet she dislikes:

"And leaves what something hidden from us chose." keeping in mind that Perloff's lines were deliberately selected for their value, while my example is finger touched at random from the poet's collected works. **33**

Cancer in my wife breast; I am eating ice cream. **34**

Wittgenstein isn't exactly correct when he says that if a lion could talk, we could not understand it. The experience of the Adamses in Africa with Elsa (and other big cats) indicates that if lions did have a language, in time and with a will to communicate and understand, we would understand them. Lions and people have a similar world of territories, mates, offspring, rearing, hunting, brain structure, body size and senses. What Wittgenstein meant was, if I understand him, is – if bacteria could speak, we could not understand them. They may already be speaking, fever a fervent appeal. **35**

We recognize that computers are making us smarter and dumber and are content with the balance as if we can afford to be in any way dumber.

"Soon, my death will be as real", he was looking around the room, "as all this."

It is a fact that on April 1, 2116, the "Centenary Brick" was removed from the corner of the Harrower (a hardscrabble town in New South Wales) municipal building to expose a small zinc time capsule which when opened showed the following contents:

1 CD-Rom with interview of 17 citizens

1 pair of sunglasses

1 can opener
1 fully sealed test tube of local water
1 fully sealed test tube of local air
1 lock of the mayor's hair
A mummified bee
1 copy of *Branches on a Wire*

The last item was testimony to a friendship that, transcending generational gaps and international borders, placed the tome with the city's councilors who, prodded by its moral and motivational messages, confronted issues with underperforming schools, local crime and a diminishing tax base, which rectified, saw Harrower rise to number 14 on *The Best Places to Retire* (Australia) ratings and my book's honored passage through time in the municipal capsule.

The poets are tired, tired of sitting at their desks, tired of rejection, tired when it comes to success, flattering and facile, tired of their own voices, all work and no recess.

The revelation of having been deceived is as distressing as the recognition of our deaths because both cases entail the destruction of the self, the one that believed, the one that lives. Liars thrive because they are allied with our most primal drive – the avoidance of pain.

"Dear Simone, the dimension of your renunciatory spiritual vision makes me giddy and the intensity of your ideas are such that they ought to be true simply from their formulation. What's a normal person to do? Here on the third planet from the sun we've spent millions of years in the lulling seas, moving from gasping lung fishes to imaginative, standing apes, princes of this world, some sky pilots, others brave doctors, master manipulators of money, a few, scholastic mystics like you, you who never enjoyed a good fuck or fine dinner, the idles of a summer afternoon or the daily responsible love for a child, pet or mate, which deeply-mildly gratifies, the closest clutch of gravity's hug that keeps us upright on the spinning globe, these you never knew."

Fine writing that was accorded an honorable mention (Foreign language tranche. English) in the 2004 biennale *Images du femme* composition competition sponsored by l'Oreal and St. Remy Brandies. Sadly, the award of a case of Remy VSOP exceeded the personal importation amount permitted by U.S. Customs.


Naked in April, bliss under the soft, cool sheets. (From *Bashed by Basho*)


We are all waiting for the catastrophe. The world system has reserves and resiliency but tolerances between normal and disaster are narrow; a small nuclear war, a big volcano, super-plague, rapid global warming could generate a set of situations that degraded us technologically by several centuries, saving us from a computer managed utopia where people don't have much to do aside from having drug enhanced orgies with erotic robots, humanity having to begin again at 1800 AD or 1000 BC, with such a bright future ahead of it.

Attend but never inwardly endorse the indictments of lovers; the accusers are axiomatically in the wrong. And if from this perspective, the appraiser seems too superior, keep in mind he or she is almost certainly going to find themselves in the same complainant position, with the localizing effect of never again being capable of such edifying neutrality. **36**

Style is not an indulgence but a transcript of fate and fate is what a person determines (in every sense) by free action. The negative proposition, the contradictory "but", the over nice emphasis on "determine", the parenthetical refinement, these are all aspects of a style. *"Style is not an indulgence but a transcript of fate and fate is what a person determines (in every sense) by free action. The negative proposition, the contradictory "but", the over nice emphasis on "determine", the parenthetical refinement, these are all aspects of a style."* [And so forth] " " " " ...

"The world doesn't lack essential structures, what's missing are compelling assemblages." – General Sir Colville-Dale, as told to Martina Hoffman in her "*Top Spin, the wit and wisdom of Henry Kissinger.*" **37**

Writing should be as fluent as speech, as talking to one's self. Even so the discourse too needs to be intricated and deepened; Henry James dictating his final quartets.

*Physics.* To have to go far down before one can reach up. What gets through to us to is the unjust hurt, showing us with the force of the never anticipated what we are.

We live at the intersection of time and space, indeed according to some philosophers, our minds constitute the conditions for time and space. A little modesty, without getting all mystical about it, might persuade us that states exist outside of time and space that, modestly considered, are not for us. In this particular, the Buddhists and Christians with their normative notions of an afterlife are correct. If such a thing is, it has to be nearly identical with what we have known, a rebirthing or a long, heavenly weekend.

My philosophy in a nut shell. Normal, everyday, ego-directed life may not be all it's cracked up to be yet it is still superior to all the destructive religious, mystical and heroic alternatives – provided you can enjoy it, and I do. Samuel Pepys over Simone Weil any day. **38**

The deer died behind the shed; it felt safe there.

Nietzsche got tired of writing lucidly and not being understood. So he figured, what the hell, write oracularly (Zarathushra) in a kind of comic bumbo-mumbo style and readers, having to overcome the resistance of the text, will be better readers for that. Like the idea that the girl who's hard to get will be more loved than the one who just puts out. Is that true? **39**

*Caveat Emptor.* I've no doubt that saints, lamas and honest mystics of the highest practice can achieve as mental realities whatever they choose to concentrate on ... Buddha in Buddha fields, Christ in glory, the kabbalistic ladder of lights. The interesting question is what the rest of us, critical spectators, uninformed consumers, are to make of it.

We were never meant for paradise, not backwards (Eden) or forward (heaven), a fact acknowledged by our deep affection for things we knock into shape, for engines that need to be kicked before they run.

Decades ago, William Stafford wrote "In Oregon, the best poets are still the coyotes." Nothing has much changed except coyotes now howl in every state. Except Hawaii.

With eons of non-existence before and after us, our lives are as brief as fireflies on a summer night. They have matured and mate in a dance of lights. Maybe they appreciate the beauty of it, maybe not; we have no idea of what it is like to be a firefly. But their lives are not too short for them. Nor ours, if we have worked, loved and made what light we can.

So what was real to this life? Inexpressible longing in adolescent for sex and love. The elation of saving lives – picking turtles off roads and catching mice in "Hav-A-Heart" traps. Some of the music of Bach, Schubert, Mahler, Brahms, Mendelssohn, Byrd, Purcell, everything by Schumann, scenes in Shakespeare, deep griefs, sex. Even if no one, no even myself, can vouch for the truth of these observancies, they are no worse than fictions that transcribe the realer than real. And at this time, we conclude our broadcast day.

*First, our national anthem.*

I never wanted sympathy, not only because I am proud but because I too have behaved badly. Granted, no one died or ended up in the hospital unless some guy spending four hours in the emergency room for just-to-be-safe x-rays counts and I guess it does. In time, I cultivated regret and made amends. Actually, the only thing I am really sorry about is not being more victorious, exactly what I expect those who injured me feel and from whom I am still waiting, if not very abidingly, an apology. This is the way we are. Low likelihood any angelic police attend our actions and if they do, it's as we watch reality TV and car crash movies, an unedifying entertainment. Have pity then for the innocent, animals, the millions murdered, the presently oppressed and not a whit for me. In the words of Mansfield Park, "The indignities of stupidity, and the disappointments of selfish passion, should excite little pity."

*Jegudiel: His pride shows insufficient reform. Phanuel: Pride is sin's strongest form. Both: Ah, how happy are we! From human passions free. How happy are we!*

Having grown up in the poor-white ghettos, without a single book in the house (not even a bible), my taste for high culture was self allegiancing and to that extent authentic. Once having found a way out from aesthetic junk space, I was never going back. Of course, we only do what we can do and that includes our self-surpassings.

Why would anyone write for the niche market of the present, the minority of the living? I write for the vastly multitudinous unborn and the judicious dead.

I write for one person in the future. You are that person. As to whom in the past, a place much more problematized with personalities, I'm inclined to name Jane Austen not that I am so proud as to be persuaded she'd find much enjoyment in my efforts. **40**

## Interview. Writer

*What has had the greatest influence on your own work?*

Since all artists invest a proper vanity in their works, their personal conceit lacks any justification. Artists who are conceited make the most basic category mistake – treating their person as art. The results are always ridiculous – Wagner in a beret or poets in capes.

*What are you currently reading? How would you describe your current project?*

The master narrative of our time is – no master narrative, encourages lot of slavish ones. Whines.

*Critics have noted the increasing compression and intensity of your work, a curtailing curve from prose to poetry to gnomic utterance. What's going on?*

Some say my aphorisms resemble used condoms. I call that a compliment.

*We live in an era of foundation funded literature, mass publicity, proliferation of literary prizes and awards even as the market for "serious" literature seems to be diminished. What are your thoughts about all that?*

Borges and Bataille are interesting in their range and second rate in their achievement. This is always the case with librarian intellectuals – browsing in the stacks has ruined their focus.

*The following is a paid poetical advertisement.*

## The Monkey God of Portals
(after the painting *A Raja Receiving Visitors*)

Another gifted hawk,
one more superfluous deer
for the over populated park.
But deference knows no doubts,
refuses the steward's lean, sufficient hand.

At moated remove from the painted palace
are the liminal precincts; roads, markets, borders
where a mounted archer notches his arrows
so nothing disrupts the declensions of greeting
unfolding like infinite silk.

For that, there's another time zone's
northern shore. A bewigged king
remembers his sleeping fleet,
slack sailed, yet straining
to fulfill a need he cannot name –
the taste of tea and long infused courtesies.

The kind of poem which written at age 20 shows promise, that at age 63 indicates benign dotage even if the words secure their usual immunity to time. This, my final poem, composed in ten minutes walking down a road, was published by the one journal I sent it to (*Writer's Eye*, 2014), earning me $50, fulfilling a life long ambition of making poetry pay. (With part of the money I bought a customized bumper-sticker, "Paid Poet".) It makes artistic symmetry to bookend this section with my only other published (in *The Blue Lantern*, 1975) poem, my first composed.

## Narcissus Chambered

Dear thin,
dear crystal friend;
I do envy him
his dense dark Cressid
who wears the Virgin's cloak
and walks without fear
the rain slick street,
her steps fresh pensees,
rainbow contusions.
Lying with my big blossomed blonde
I hear and bruise her
bouquets of yellow pansies
to pale his lurid verse
and make her sleep uneasy
dreaming of me.

Within the correlative margins of a life, it is easy to discern an evolution from gnomic, hypercompressed lyric to Audenesque meditative vade mecum, a mediated vectoring that the poems' juxtaposition on the page refutes as non-collaborative distancing, definitive enough provided the four forces of vox – the high-minded, the declarative, the bitter and the blokeish-jokish are recognized as the determinate physical parameters.

# Readers' Advisory

Brachiumetalicum ("Branches on a Wire") is aphorismic agent with prosaic supplementation applied optically for the treatment of mild mental hypo-stimulation and affiliated disorders. Take only as directed. Tell your metaphysician if you drink alcohol as alcohol is an aphorismic enhancer. Dosages exceeding ten units a day (or less if enhanced) may result in headache, nausea, diurnal dreaming and revulsion. Rectal cramp, foot fidgets, "wandering eye", increased TV-urge may be signs of boredom, a serious reactive condition. Suspend Brachiumetalicum intake and administer a lexical affect moderator, such as Readers' Digest Condensed or WSJ ("Wall Street Journal"). Brachiumetalicum is a general spectrum ameliorative and should not be prescribed for hypo or hyper pedagogued patients or those diagnosed with aphorismic allergies, Cioran Reflux or Nietzsche's Megalomania (and its precursors). Do not take while driving or operating heavy machinery. Rare occurrences of risus lachrymose have been reported. In the event of laughter and crying, discontinue Brachiumetalicum immediately and consult a clinical cognition or other health professional.

# Notes

*1.* Shot or shout, tribes on the borders, smoke in the west and the morning's menace.

*2.* I was on a slightly (b)elated honeymoon with my second (and current) )wife, Laurie Kim, a highly intelligent and energetic woman ten years my junior, an accomplished software designer for a library systems firm. Well educated in the American way, she has little knowledge of high culture, while respecting it, being Korean-American, so that her remark, leaving the Ritterholm ... "that was weird" struck me as utterly apposite – the white, plastered over brick interior, the thin chill light, the massive marble tombs scattered about like derailed box cars, with Latin epithets in black inset metallic letters, a mounted shield or pike, the gashed breastplate where a life bled out, yes weird was the right word for that terminus for pale kings killed in anonymous northern wars, cold, cold, and very old, its iron spike pinning Gamla Stam's twisted, living streets, the quay side shops glittering with trays of amber that had trapped the tiny flies.

*3.* Suddenly, we were in a different element, one of passage, transport, flight, of hot engines, thrust, danger, the glint of metals, our bodies utterly able, clothes off, lift off.

*4.* It took an American (Twain) to get it right. "Wagner's music is not as bad as it sounds."

*5.* First, allow me to crush you, pity will follow. Stop murdering and we will abolish the death penalty right away. Thank you for your Christmas gift of two viles: self-pity and hate.

**6.** The next step, a book that is wholly an index, has not only been thought of but almost certainly already achieved, with further post-postmodern effect achieved by gradually reintroducing "the text"

**7.** I too have known the demeaning vanity of having a name. It would be better for poets to take the designation of fruits. It is hard to get puffed up with a name like "Peach" "Apple" or even the more acerbic "Lime" especially since in this crowded world a number would be needed for specificity. "It is an honor to introduce our distinguished reader this evening, Banana 5,856."

**8.** The best biographies are still external surveys even as they describe habits of mind (Holroyd's *Strachey*, for instance), the view is still from outside. Only criticism gives interior access, a "life" of thought, though it isn't really biography since the focus "quantumizes" the object of its study.

**9.** In my own work I've tried to avoid this, not by trying to put good content in good forms – the obvious blue print for another failure – but by putting not good into the not good though this misses the evasive subtlety of it (the sorta not good into ... etc.), a self subverting project that makes an ad hoc arrangement of various "not to trues" that is oppositionally supporting, a lean-to, an aluminum shack shining amid vast suburban tracts of predictable ambitions.

**10.** "Are there still works that distinguish themselves sufficiently from the general run of things, from banality, to merit the name of art?" (Jean Baudrillard, *Fragments*, p.85).

    Yes, good work can and does surface but it is quickly neutralized and becomes complicit with the system. The art-system exists to produce "art" as marketable commodity, 95% of it junk of the easily imbibed kind we all enjoy and 5% indigestible "art-art" that criticizes itself (and the system) as nullity (rather than banality), an auto- immune response. These objects crucially mimic the essential quality of great art, its non-consumability (great art isn't ever consumable; it consumes the perceiver); they are properly useless, like the Emperor's new clothes, only viable/visible as manifestations of intellectual and financial power.

For facilitating this bit of rhetoric, my thanks to Andy Warhol for the loan of his soap box. The show is over; the show must go on.

**11.** Subjects in experiment, asked to invent a song or supply verbal associations, invent less after exposure to a concluded work than one interrupted.

**12.** I was fortunate that my primary care physician recognized the persistent symptoms of vertigo, joint pain and fatigue required deeper diagnostics, referring me to the nearby University of Virginia Medical Center. A battery of test over three weeks finally yielded an answer. I was suffering from Colfax-Marlowe Disease, a rare heliapontic disorder affecting no more than 10,000 persons world wide, chiefly in the Northern hemisphere. "CM" as it is called, is a disruption in the body's aspastic hormonal-dyronal secretion and uptake system. Typical diagnostic indicators are reduced torine levels, caused by blockades in the triangular nexus and/or low production in Islets of Lingerhans marked by high octide oxygenation when not accompanied by lympetoic atrophy. Low kalen levels, as measured by fast-hydrogen beam spectrography may also be present. Long term prognosis for patients used to be poor and treatment was palliative. But recent advances in genetic medicine (especially the development of specific micro-synthetic tytactic factors) can stop the disease's progress, in some cases indefinitely and further advances may promise permanent remission or cure. As Dr Jason Doby, my specialist physician at NIH-Remote, remarked "Mr Nelson, I'd say we are probably good until at least 2020 – and we'll take it from there."

Yea, I was grateful (at 80% covered, 20% deductible) yet thought if you (Dr Doby) could prevent my inevitable death or raise the dead, then were your profession more estimable.

**13.** The Aztecs had the advantage over the Norse in terms of warrior retirement. Instead of carousing in the mead hall, Aztec warriors of merit were reborn as eternal hummingbirds.

**14.** Zizek is right on this issue. Every desire may be criticized as vain, false, illusionary, unworthy, indeed harmful. Yet the place of desire (always occupied by something) is constitutive and what makes us human.

**15.** At the extreme were those last hold outs of the imperial army who remained unsurrendered in the jungles for decades, even after reading leaflets dropped by Japanese authorities, with photos and pleas from the families for them to give up. The leaflets were closely scrutinized and minor flaws in letter inking or character spacing were taken as proofs that the appeals were propaganda efforts by the desperate Americans who even with spies in Japan were losing.

*Pacific Bathic*

*A reconnaissance team, we were landed to watch the straits. No relief came. On the airwaves, tiny words,*

*English, Japanese interweaved.*
*Dial lights dimmed. After many bright days, rain.*

*Iwo died from fever. Saito complained of cramps.*
*He set out for the mainland on a driftwood plank.*

*Weeks, months, the knot slipped down the calendar stick.*
*Each year, I place a stone upon the silent shine, the radio.*
*I check the fish lines, levels in the water barrels.*
*The surf beats. Days and nights I try to sleep.*

*Today, a tower breaks the misty band of sea and sky.*
*A merchant ship beyond the reef. Plainly painted on its prow,*
*our flag's red and white. My hands three times rise*
*"Banzai, Banzai Banzai."*

*The war had gone far from here. It stayed in my dreams,*
*mixed with women and a newsreel I'd seen.*
*The Emperor riding a stallion became the sun rising,*
*sacred Nippon.*
*Black rays reached across the ocean to our Co-prosperity*
*zone!*

*All morning I have watched the sailors scamble like*
*crabs, like lice.*
*The launched boat nears. I sweep the radio top clear.*

*Years are islands, stones sparkle in the sand.*

**16.** The time comes when patients find their physicians pathetic, working so hard on a project (preserving life) the possessors no longer care about. Still the doctors are professionals and must be allowed their practice. One recalls the old joke: an elderly man complains to his doctor "I can't pee." The doctor asks the standard diagnostic questions and "How old are you?" The man says eighty. The doctor looks thoughtful and says "Haven't you pee'd enough?" The joke is obviously and doubly "displaced." The man is really complaining he can't ejaculate. ("Haven't you fucked enough?") The man is complaining about any ailment ("Haven't you lived enough?").

**17.** The vast majority of aphorisms, even the classics by Rochefoucauld and Nietzsche, are utterly unmemorable because in their explicitness they lack the strange element ("deep poetry") that would make them really real. As in life, the esoterics (lamas, mystics, Lacanians) are right. Something uncanny underlies reality, call it karma, ming, fate or, my term, the petit fuckit a. The aphorism, trying to be a good semantic citizen, lacks the petit fuckit a.

Wittgenstein remarks "Raisins may be the best part of the cake; but a bag of raisins is not better than cake; someone who gives us a bag of raisins maybe cannot bake with them. I am thinking of aphorisms". (*Culture and Value*, p. 76.) Very true but a week of fine cake will spoil one for that delight while one may get pleasantly habituated to a handful of raisins as daily ration. They have become a raison d'etre, French for "reason to eat."

**18.** "The choice of permanent silence doesn't negate the artist's work. On the contrary, it imparts retroactively an added power and authority, denial of the work becoming a new source of its validity, a certification of unchallengeable seriousness ... the truly serious attitude is one that regards art as something that can best be achieved only by abandoning it ...". Susan Sontag, *Styles of Radical Will*. Or as Wittgenstein remarked, "In art, it is often better to do nothing than anything at all." For many ailments, the best drug is Placebo.

**19.** The interesting about "near death encounters" is how nobody on the other side has anything interesting to say to the newly arrived. The conversations are all at the level of a genealogical convention: "Meet the grandma you never knew.", "Here's your dad" and it is never as interesting as "My dad – my uncle you mean?", "No, your dad, really." The testifiers we hear from have all chosen to go back to life and who can blame them given the alternative – an eternity of family reunion tedium.

**20.** Why Laertes is a better friend to Hamlet than Horatio.

**21.** My formal contribution to world literature is the referenced aphorism or footnoted paralipomenon. Possibly, someone French (Oulipo?) was first, not that annotated school editions of the great maxim-makers would count. The object was to add dimensionally to this quintessentially short form. The items in Branches on a Wire maybe read in standard "horizontal" page to page scansion even as they propose a "vertical" reading mandated by the indicative endnotes. The fact that the sections do not face each other across the page, a possibility, but are separated by sectionalization, constitutes a caesura, with important aesthetic implications that at the moment elude me. The title however is suggestive. May I add, having the responsibility of sustaining the viability of this verbal form throughout the English speaking world is an onerous burden.

**22.** Just technically, she had relinquished a quota of her jouissance in the Lacandian sense to enter the symbolic order, myself enjoying her in ways that implied I was getting more out of it than her (though she appeared to me get a lot out of it!), possessing as the Other, her sacrificed portion. She needed to get her own back ("revenge") by transgressing "the master's" imposed norms. I am grateful to Zizek (*The Plague of Fantasies*) for this engaging fairly tale.

23. As I always say, "On est quelquefois moins malheureux d'être trompé de ce qu'on aime, que d'en être détrompé."

24. Perhaps dreams are the Real and "reality", old news from psychiatry, the fantasy.

    Elsewhere, literature is consciously constructed in the light assembly suburbs that surround the dream factory which processes the raw material and sets the basic form.

    One would be remiss, knowing of it, not to exhibit Samuel Pepys' extraordinary dream of the Aug, 15th, 1665. "Something put my last night's dream into my head, which I think was the best that ever was dreamed – which was, that I had my Lady Castlemayne in my armes and was admitted to use all the dalliance I desired with her, and then dreamed that this could not be awake but that it was only a dream. But that since it was a dream and that I took such so much real pleasure in it, what a happy thing it would be, if when we are in our graves (as Shakespear resembles it), we could dream and dream such dreams as this – that then we should not seem so fearful of death as we are in this dread plague time."

25. The best motive for literary writing, as identified by some clear minded 18th century type, Dr Johnson or Sheridan, is fame and fortune. Considerably poorer ones are self comprehension and self-expression, the seemingly superior moral status of the former devalued when one realizes it amounts to nothing more than self expression **for one**. At best, writing is a poor means for self understanding, a

path to unpurposed destinations as I came to see when various harsh and supercilious observations surfaced that were special effects unrepresentative of my living attitude (which has generally and genially been contended, tolerant and conscientious), excrescences incubated by the strange chemistries of writing that were in no sense festering presences prodded by a probe. I have always known that the reason for writing is to tell truth and create beauty, these achieved once or twice though now they flee from me that sometimes did me seek.

26. After writing this, I discover a similar if better expressed opinion of St Simone's, "When we think we have a choice, it is because we are unconscious, we cease to be toys of life when we abandon our willful illusions and recognize necessity, there is then no longer any choice, a certain action is imposed by the situation itself—clearly perceived."

27. The thing you least desire is, by your very fixation, the thing you most desire.

28. In terms of happiness, some think it's all down hill from the womb.

29. These distractions can be purely neurotic or "artistic". In the words of Burroughs [his introduction to *Queer*], "I would never have become a writer but for shooting my wife, I live with the constant threat of possession, a constant need to escape. The death of Joan maneuvered me into a life long struggle, in which I have no choice except to write my way out." Let us note: in Burroughs's creative variation, he was the perp, not the victim.

The injury, if it is not so damaging as to pre-empt identity, endows a deeper perspective by undermining narcissism's light body of well-being. One acquires weight and gravitas. The instant it is positivized by such a reflection, its functional value is mitigated to the status of just another asset. To work it's transformative power, the injury must be desublimated, reenergized and reactivated into a present painfulness that is non-negotiable and destructive. Insight happens in transition and at a glance, like an instant of relief just before you think, falsely as it turns out, it is relief.

**30.** Gorie Jraham Disease is a progressive-degenerative disorder affecting writers, chiefly in the United States. Symptoms are dysenteric expression, prolixity and acute atrophy of the selfcensorius decorum. Approximately 300 cases are diagnosed each year. The disease takes decades to run its course, with a mortality rate of 110%. While there is no cure, there is mope. Send your dontorations to Stop Gorie Jraham Disease, Boylston Hall, Harvard University, Cambridge MA, 22401. All contrabulations are tax deducible."

This was the medicinal jape that broke the camel's back, the camel being my old collaborator, William Ruminant who truth to tell does have a stolid solid dromedariel dignity. Because truth to tell, I had sent this manuscript to Ruminate at WRITES despite the issues (cited in the acknowledgments) with his prior work, my A Book of Emblems. A few weeks later, he called me.

"Look the jokes have got to go. They're not funny. Most of them are mean. They mar the book." He heard my intake of breath and continued. "Hear me out. Take the Jorie Graham joke. It's juvenile, like your son appearing at breakfast with a ring through his nose and burping. Look, she's a serious artist, doing her long line consciousness and conscience thing. Give her a break.

Drop the jokes, all of them."

"You mean give you a break. I've got a list, two pages legal pad of stuff you screwed up on Emblems. It's for its, your for you're, wrong dashes, football as two words. Let me get the list." He sighed.

"There's a lot going on here now. They killed the Veterinary School and that was one of Edmister's originals. They figured the animals couldn't complain. No alum network." He sad-snorted. "All the money is going to the new business school. It's all about Edmister University's School of Business and International Finance. They wanna put WRITES on the chopping block. I offered them an edition of the Hoosier Homer, James Whitcomb Reilly. So yeah, we've been distracted. Send me the list."

I could sense his weariness and it's a fact, show weakness and guys go in for the kill. Guys with a grievance anyway and I had two pages worth. So I said "And you'll find time for a new edition and Whitcomb Reilly AFTER they let you edit their biz magazine?"

Seriously, you ought to be able to embezzle $250 K from a university without anybody ever noticing and if you aren't smart enough to do that why are you even there? Meantime, you're up at the green board, hams on view like the biggest baddest roo-boomer, turning significantly interrogatively as you track down that Heideggerian mammoth of meaning and music, the semi-colon, spot lighted by 14 eyes in seven feminine headsets, liquid and luminous, flash fired by overworked limbic circuits; radar and contra radar, your gaze infiltrates theirs to lodge n the seat of Venus (their amygdala), your manikin holographed in the beam – See, he ascends, conducting like Stokowski or Goebbels sturm surges of Transference. Me, all my women were earned by the free affirmation of mature minds. Now I'm not saying Ruminant did any thing wrong, just recalling an old country proverb –

> One man murders grammar,
> One man murders his wife.
> One man.

**31.** This statement, recorded on the backs of innumerable cereal boxes, is attributed to Cornfusius.

**32.** Granted, one should allow some leeway for a book honestly sub-titled (spoiler!) *reflections of a damaged life*. Bro Adorno, the problem is you paint with too broad a brush, exactly what you of all people should avoid. "Even the blossoming tree lies the moment its bloom is seen without the shadow of terror." A remark that resembles a drama queen's shriek, given this was written in spring of 1945 in California where you are having a good war when mission number one for you and Horkheimer should have been the extraction of Benjamin from France via job permit. Granted he was reluctant to go, would miss the Bib Nationale, would almost certainly embarrass you and your American hosts by drinking, gambling and pinching women – specifically Mrs. Adorno. Benjamin abroad was convenient. So go ahead, take your time, criticize the complacent American trees, take the whole "nature industry" to task and while you're at it, let Benjamin die.

**33.** "roast potatoes for" is by Gertrude Stein; "staging rockets may", never encountered by Perloff, is a six second (one to imagine, five to type) slight of hand by Page Nelson. The longer opposing line is by Philip Larkin. If this exercise seems too ludic and self-indulgent, this is exactly the style of Perloff approved Bernstein and other "abstract writers" such as Howe and Goldsmith. Poetic allegiance is never as obvious as it may appear; my poem "Blue", the four letter word centered alone on a white sea of sheet, is generally considered to be one of the finest "abstract" productions of the last fifty years, being pure, definitive if vastly implicative, every word of it an island connected to the main. To give Goldsmith his due, he understands that the weight of writing reached critical mass a long time ago, exploding before anyone noticed into a background of low energy frivolity, about 3.4 reads or .5 writes (every other American being a writer) per annum.

**34.** It's true, I want to do my wife's oncologist. She is small, with perfect legs. Maybe she was born to have them, maybe she works out. Are they too perfect for perfection? Alchemical priestess of the infusion room, she is firm but upbeat, responsibly just short of cheerful. She doesn't let death get her down. For me to get her down, to see her in the little death of her climax would be to share somehow in her existential-transactional triumph. Meantime, wife's health is so-so, that is, her prognosis is good.

**35.** Dr Stanislaw Lem was the world leader in research on communicating microorganisms.

**36.** The eminent detective Philip Marlowe never took divorce cases.

**37.** Ineffective as even weird humour, the author's aim, aside from forthright effrontery may be in assertion that the improbability of such an improbability consists of the improbable configuration of the current, all history to the present moment. Napoleon might have won the battle of Waterloo (but not by atomic weapons). I find nothing perverse in a British general's philosophical remarks recorded in a popular author's compilation of sayings by the borsch belt comedian of American state craft other than the braggadocio of the assertion suggesting an indictment that such things should exist at all, nominally implicating that anything should exist at all, resembling the person, surely more condonable than condemnable, who persistently insists on being ignored.

***38.*** About misery St. Simone is never wrong. "Feeling of impossibility, situations in which the imagination which moulds fictitiously the past, the future cannot succeed in filling up the voids. It tries and fails. Arrested impetus. When suffering has reached the point where the imagination which manufactures compensations can no longer function, inward oscillations between refusal and acceptance. An enforced void. After a long time, there follows exhaustion and death of parts of the soul." (*Notebook*, Vol. 1, p. 198)

***39.*** Which is rather the point of these damn footnotes, to disrupt the simple passage of a linear reading when the book wants nothing more than to speak clearly and forthrightly, a fine thing for daily discourse but art taking life itself for its subject requires a deeper grammar and syntax more intricate, even if as often the case, it strives for the appearance of simplicity. And so this book fails, trying too hard, not resting where it should, a failure backwards and forwards, up and down and yet for all that staking out a position that contests the siege of time with no expectation of admiration or endurance.

This broadly bifurcated exposition formally exhibits the fissure in my being, separating my aspiration and my achievements, my hope and my history, my best intentions and my actual deeds. Most people inhabit a similar terrain even as its personal texture is distinctly individual. In my case "the brake" is always twilight, windless with an air of immanence; under a *View of Toledo* sky, a gray featureless moraine of shale that sinks under foot and fills in to the ankles. A backward glance reverts one to the usual suburbs of daily obligations and interests; instead one slogs forward to reach that impossible place of enhanced perceptions, powers and pleasures we had a sense of when young and in love only now, for all our efforts, we're not getting there. This is the shadow land; Desire.

[As to the obdurate girl, a distinguished philologist (Werner Hamacher) has written, "the disconcerting can be loved, only the beloved that resists enduringly desired" which is hogwash but in the words of S.J. Perelman, don't you wish you could wash a hog like that? Concerning Perelman, when one is mooded to suppose intelligence the most important quality a prose writer can posses, he exists to realize your bias, cogitating at the top of the heap, with so many pistons firing you think his mind a biochemical V-16, twice the normal V-8, if you know what I mean. The only problem is one can only go so far with him, not comfortable (accustomed to the normal lexical Studebakers) with such a powerful (and refined) machine, as if you were using a Lamborghini for the weekly grocery haul, the kind of sentiment Perelman could express in nine words you'd remember and laugh at too.]

**40.** Despite the excellencies of Austen's style, most Americans will be progressively disappointed by her failure to present carriage crashes and duellos in real ratios characteristic of her society both as narrative objects and as iconic representations of the violence inherit in the system which she refuses to objectify as dead bodies.

# Afterwords

My sincerest hope is that the reader's encounter with this volume (a short one will do) would leave him or her not edified, entertained or beautified ("a vile phrase"), for there exists a superplus of literary engenderers (read Shakespeare, Keats, Dickens, Austen …) but with a sensation like a holly prick or berry pip between the teeth, contact with a item not pliant, incontestably real, like yourself, brief if durant, not a great thing nor a small one either.

If betrayal has been a theme of this book, it has been presented not as whine but as work of research. For much that is wrong in the world can be construed as betrayal; cancer, a plane crash, (mechanical failures of all kinds), a surgeon' s mistake, bank closures, politics leading to war, the destruction of the environment. On one account, it all begins with betrayal: Adam and Eve betray god who first betrayed them by presenting an irresistible temptation. A treacherous lover has an important role but is of no more significance than one of those private tutors who instructs you in a language with a vast literature. In this case, the corpus is history (everything that has *just* happened).

I often think of those photographs from the early days of the Lodz ghetto, the newly weds, parents with young children, all smiling in the hope of life. The war looks to go on and on and everyone knows the Nazis need workers; as long as you work, you will live. Now who would disappoint or shall I say betray such a reasonable expectation?

The rest is silence.

# Index

**A**

Adorno, Theodor
 *19, 72, 90, 99, 136*
art *passim*
Austen, Jane *119, 139, 141*

**B**

Basho *139, 141*
Bataille, Georges *74, 121*
Baudrillard, Jean
 *26, 35, 74, 126*
Bellow, Saul *29*
Benjamin, Walter *19, 136*
Boleyn, Anne *107*
Borges, Jorge *121*
Burroughs, William *133*

**C**

Caesar
 *19, 30, 31, 38, 39, 49*
Canetti, Elias *76, 79*
Carsen, John *5, 6, 18*
Cioran, Emil *27, 124*

**D**

Dalai Lama *25*
Donne, John *37*

**H**

Hegel, Frederick *87*
Henry VIII *107*

**I**

index *143*

**J**

James, Henry *116*

**K**

Kim, Laurie *104, 125*
Kimmel, Husband (admiral)
 *88*

**L**

Lacan, Jacques *73, 74, 76*
Lee, R. E. *46, 100*
Lowell, Robert
 *vii, 19, 91, 107*

**M**

Malvolio (character) *47, 86*

**N**

Nielsen, Judyta
 *iv, 6, 13, 15, 16*
Nietzsche, Frederick
 *19, 69, 117, 124, 130*

**P**

Perelman, S. J. *106, 139*
Perloff, Marjorie *111, 136*
Pinter, Harold *64*
poetry *passim*
Pompey the Great *30, 38*

**R**

Raine, Kathleen *81, 83*
Ruminant, William
 *21, 134, 136*

**S**

Schumann, Robert *96, 118*
sex *passim*
Shakespeare, William *passim*
Sitwell, Sacheverell *19*

**T**
Thucydides *70*

**U**
Updike, John *18*, *29*

**W**
Wagner, Richard
    *25*, *120*, *125*
Wallbane, Baxter *1*, *102*
Weil, Simone *99*, *116*
Wittgenstein, Ludwig
    *94*, *95*, *110*, *112*, *130*
writers, writing *passim*

**Z**
Zolduck, Hiram *20*, *110*

www.ingramcontent.com/pod-product-compliance
Lightning Source LLC
Chambersburg PA
CBHW032134040426
42449CB00005B/231